JAPANESE
GARDEN DESIGN
TRADITIONS AND TECHNIQUES

JAPANESE GARDEN DESIGN
TRADITIONS AND TECHNIQUES

An inspiring history of the classical gardens of Japan and a
study of their distinctive characteristics and design features

Charles Chesshire

southwater

This edition is published by Southwater
an imprint of Anness Publishing Ltd
Blaby Road, Wigston
Leicestershire LE18 4SE
Email: info@anness.com

Web: www.southwaterbooks.com;
www.annesspublishing.com

If you like the images in this book and would like
to investigate using them for publishing,
promotions or advertising, please visit our website
www.practicalpictures.com for more information.

Publisher: Joanna Lorenz
Editorial Director: Helen Sudell
Project Editor: Emma Clegg
Designers: Simon Daley and Mike Morey
Jacket design: Nigel Partridge
Additional materials and equipment
   text: Jenny Hendy
Illustrators: Anna Laflin and
   Anna Koska
Special photography (locations and
   steps): Alex Ramsay
Special photography (materials and
   equipment): Peter Anderson
Production Controller: Christine Ni

© Anness Publishing Ltd 2011

A CIP catalogue record for this book is available
from the British Library.

Previously published as part of a larger volume,
Japanese Gardening.

ETHICAL TRADING POLICY
At Anness Publishing we believe that business
should be conducted in an ethical and
ecologically sustainable way, with respect for the
environment and a proper regard to the
replacement of the natural resources we employ.
As a publisher, we use a lot of wood pulp in high-
quality paper for printing, and that wood
commonly comes from spruce trees. We are
therefore currently growing more than 750,000
trees in three Scottish forest plantations. The
forests we manage contain more than 3.5 times
the number of trees employed each year in
making paper for the books we manufacture.
Because of this ongoing ecological investment
programme, you, as our customer, can have the
pleasure and reassurance of knowing that a tree is
being cultivated on your behalf to naturally
replace the materials used to make the book you
are holding. For further information about this
scheme, go to www.annesspublishing.com/trees

Contents

Introduction

"Visualize the famous landscapes of our country and come to understand their most interesting points. Recreate the essence of these scenes in the garden, but do so interpretatively, not strictly."

From the *Sakuteiki*, the earliest known book of Japanese garden design, written in the 11th century.

Left: *Water plays a crucial role in Japanese gardens. This waterfall at St Mawgan, in Cornwall, England, is designed to look naturally formed as in nature. The source of the water is well hidden amongst the lush foliage of bamboo.*

The Japanese garden has captured the imagination of Western gardeners ever since they discovered its delights in the 19th century. Japan, isolated from the rest of the world from the 1630s to over 200 years later, had been nurturing extraordinary and unique styles of architecture, poetry, painting, flower arranging and gardening. When artists, architects and designers in the West were finally exposed to these Japanese arts in the late 19th century, they were astonished by what they found.

The strong influence of Japanese arts is still being felt today. Of these arts, Japanese garden design, in particular, exerts a powerful and mystical grip. Steeped in significance and refinement, the Japanese garden has enormous appeal, especially for landscape designers seeking both a deeper meaning and a more contemporary edge for their own work.

THE STYLES OF JAPANESE GARDENS

Japanese landscape gardens can be categorized into five main styles – pond gardens, dry gardens, tea gardens, stroll gardens and courtyard gardens – and each of these has a long and intimate relationship with the history of Japan. Even a modest knowledge of Japanese history, especially the country's relationship with China and Buddhism, will go a long way towards helping us to understand the art of the Japanese garden, and thereby enabling us to reproduce it.

It was the dynamic, creative energies of Zen monks and painters of the medieval period that set the stage for the development of the exceptional art form that is the Japanese garden. These ancient gardens, especially those constructed of stone and sand (some of which survive even from the 15th century), have become the benchmark of abstract garden art throughout the world.

THE SIGNIFICANCE OF PLANTS

Plants are fundamental to all but a few Japanese gardens. Most of the plants used possess symbolic significance, including the twisted pine, scattered cherry blossom, pendulous wisteria, the lotus ('purity rising out of the mud') and fiery Japanese maple. These plants are always placed with restraint and care, and gardeners celebrate the seasons through their fleeting beauty. Everything in the garden – plants, rocks, lanterns, water – serves a role in the creation of a unified, harmonious and poetic picture. This is an art in which the whole is far greater than the sum of its parts.

Right: *A patchwork of different species of moss in the dappled sunshine at Sanzen-in, Ohara, near Kyoto. The soft velvet carpets of moss under Japanese cedars (Cryptomeria) produce a magical effect.*

THE SIGNIFICANCE OF WATER AND ROCKS

Water is one of the most important elements in the Japanese garden. It can often be found in the form of a pond, a stream or a simple small water basin. Even when water is absent, its presence is often suggested through areas of sand and gravel, or dry streams. Rocks are equally important and are regarded as possessing a kind of spiritual and living essence that needs to be respected if they are to be placed successfully.

A real understanding of the two elements of rock and water, through careful observation in nature, will help to form a good basis for creating Japanese-style gardens. The more the "natural law" of these elements is understood, the easier it becomes to treat them in abstract ways.

It is this abstraction of nature that is most difficult to reproduce successfully in a garden. But don't be put off: it is perfectly possible to assimilate some of the simple beauty of Japanese gardens without delving into the often esoteric meaning behind them.

HOW TO USE THIS BOOK

This book shows you how to create a beautiful and individual Japanese garden that fulfils the exacting criteria set down by centuries of Japanese garden designers and philosophers. The first two chapters explain the history of this unique gardening style and show how it has evolved to become a precise art form that has been inspired and influenced by environmental and cultural elements, in particular Zen, and attitudes and

Left: *Statues of the Buddha are not common in Japanese gardens, but this one makes up part of an entrancing collection assembled in a forest of bamboo by the early 20th-century artist Hashimoto Kansetsu.*

beliefs concerning the natural world. This section also describes ways in which the principles have been interpreted over the years, and suggests how you might continue this tradition by adapting them. The five main garden styles (pond, dry, tea, stroll and courtyard) are then outlined in their traditional forms so you can see the differences and similarities between them. A garden plan for each style is supplied, which explains the key elements of each. Chapters on Natural Materials, Creative Constructs and Water Features introduce essential elements, supported by practical explanations of how to achieve them. Together they guide you through the process of designing a Japanese garden.

A HISTORY OF JAPANESE GARDENING

The story of this gardening tradition is both long and fascinating. Understanding its history and learning about the people who were involved in its development gives an insight into the philosophy that inspires the Japanese garden. With such knowledge, we can plan and create gardens in this style with confidence and conviction. Although the essential style of Japanese gardens can be imitated simply by copying their outward form and appearance, reproducing their spirit requires a much deeper understanding.

The following chapter leads us through the main Japanese historical periods, made distinct by wave after wave of Chinese and Buddhist influences. These have combined with the Japanese people's strong sense of self, and their glorious landscape and native religion, to produce the uniquely curious and beautiful art form that is the Japanese garden. It is remarkable that garden styles from over 1,000 years ago still inform today's gardens. Even in the most avant-garde modern gardens you can often find motifs from Heian romanticism, the dry gardens of the Muromachi period or the tea gardens of the Momoyama period.

Above: *A chequerboard of stone squares sunk into a sea of moss.*
Left: *A tea house at Saiho-ji Moss Temple in Kyoto.*

The evolution of the garden

There are six important periods in the history of the Japanese garden, most of them coinciding with dramatic changes in Japan's history. The division into six is an oversimplification, but it helps to explain the evolution of some of the distinct styles of these gardens. Each period is defined not only by the practicalities and customs of contemporary Japanese life, but also by the conflicts and changes brought by religion, culture, politics and warfare. Chinese artistic influence was strong, and Buddhism brought a sense of spirituality to Japanese garden design.

Above: *A garden of clipped shrubs, which are known as* o-karikomi, *at Sanzen-in, a garden from the Edo period.*

THE DIFFERENT PERIODS

As recently as the 1970s, a garden from the 9th century was excavated in Nara. The history of the Japanese garden really starts at that time, now known as the Nara period. It continues through the five subsequent periods – the 11th-century Heian period, the 13th-century Kamakura period, the 15th-century Muromachi period, the 16th-century Momoyama period (which all centred around the old capital of Kyoto), and lastly the 18th- and 19th-century Edo period (after the capital moved to Tokyo). The gardens of the 20th century are more complex in their style and are dealt with later under "Modern and Western influences".

NARA PERIOD (710–94)

A period of pond and stream gardens, and gardens for ceremonies (Chinese Tang dynasty, 618–906)
Built in 710, Nara, which lies some 48km (30 miles) south of Kyoto, was the last of the ancient capitals of Japan. Excavations in 1974 found vestiges of an ornamental garden on the site of an old palace. They revealed a winding stream, edged in gravel and pebbles in a naturalistic style, with unique, sophisticated rock arrangements. These gardens were almost certainly used for ceremonial purposes, and were quite similar to those that were constructed in China during the same period.

HEIAN PERIOD (794–1185)

The first wave of Chinese influence and Pure Land Paradise gardens (Chinese Tang dynasty, 618–906; Five Dynasties, 906–60; Chinese Song dynasty, 960–1279)
This, the most romantic period in Japanese cultural history, saw a great many refinements, and also showed a new sensitivity to detail and a focus on the seasons and rituals, all of which evolved under imperial rule in Kyoto. One of the key features was the creation of pond and island gardens that reproduced the Mystic Isles of the immortals and the Pure Land Paradise garden of Buddha Amida, into which the souls of the pure could be reborn after death.

Another new feature was the garden design that enabled court ceremonies, music and poetry readings to be performed in courtyards, on boats and by the side of streams. The *Sakuteiki*, possibly the world's first great garden treatise, was written during this period in the 11th century.

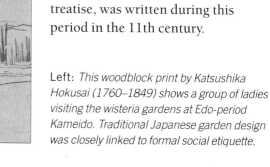

Left: *This woodblock print by Katsushika Hokusai (1760–1849) shows a group of ladies visiting the wisteria gardens at Edo-period Kameido. Traditional Japanese garden design was closely linked to formal social etiquette.*

KAMAKURA PERIOD (1185–1392)

The second wave of Chinese influence with the arrival of Zen (Chinese Song dynasty, 960–1279; Yuan or Mongol dynasty, 1279–1368; Chinese Ming dynasty, 1368–1644) Minamoto was the first *shogun* (military dictator) in Japan, and his government, based in Kamakura, took little interest in the arts until Buddhist monks began returning from China bringing tea, paintings of the Song dynasty and early artefacts of the Ming dynasty. They were also influenced by the Zen Buddhism of China. The imperial family in Kyoto continued with the same traditions as in the Heian period. Around 1339, the Saiho-ji and Tenryu-ji gardens were created in Kyoto, inspired by scenes from Song-dynasty paintings. Zen monks started to make gardens, and rocks became an important element.

MUROMACHI PERIOD (1393–1568)

The era of the devastating Onin wars and the refining influence of Zen on garden-making (Chinese Ming dynasty, 1368–1644)

The mingling of the warrior classes with the imperial classes in Kyoto led to an extraordinary flowering of the arts. This period saw the building of the Golden Pavilion in the 1390s and the Silver Pavilion in the 1470s by Ashikaga shoguns, whose pond-filled stroll gardens were a departure from the earlier preference for boating lakes. The most important innovation of this period was the creation of "dry water" gardens (*kare-sansui*) that used rocks set in gravel or sand to symbolize water. The designs of these gardens were influenced by Zen Buddhism and the black and white ink landscape paintings. The most famous of these gardens are the Daisen-in (made in about 1513) and the Ryoan-ji (1499).

Right: The Golden Pavilion in Kyoto, which is covered in gold leaf, was built in the 1390s by the first of the Ashikaga shoguns, marking the beginning of the Muromachi period.

MOMOYAMA PERIOD (1568–1603)

The era of the unifiers who would build Japan as a single nation and the rise of the tea masters and the merchant class (Chinese Ming dynasty, 1368–1644)

Three successive military unifiers built gardens using far larger rocks than before, designed as an expression of power, but this excess was also tempered by the modesty of an important new feature: the tea house and garden. The famous tea-ceremony ritual was initially popularized by a merchant called Rikyu, who was one of the most influential figures in Japan.

Above: The gardens around Nijo Castle, in Kyoto, were constructed at the beginning of the Edo period. These gardens used larger rocks than ever before and in greater numbers.

EDO PERIOD (1603–1867)

The era of National Isolation and the private stroll gardens (Chinese Qing dynasty, 1644–1911)

In 1603, the Tokugawa shogunate moved to the eastern capital, Edo (now Tokyo), where strict social structures were enforced. The gardens of this period are characterized by stroll gardens, the most famous being the Katsura Detached Palace, in Kyoto. With its many pond-side tea houses and buildings, and exquisite framed views, it might represent the last great peak in large-scale Japanese garden art.

Meanwhile, wealthy city merchants and samurai developed the small courtyard garden, incorporating motifs from the dry gardens and the tea gardens of earlier ages. In time, gardens became more ostentatious, losing the creative edge and philosophical depth of their predecessors. Since 1867, however, when Japan reopened its borders to the West, gardens have explored the minimalism of Zen and more avant-garde and naturalistic styles, although still incorporating traditional motifs such as the Mystic Isles.

Waves of Chinese influence

Before AD607, Japan was a primitive culture that had received only a trickle of Chinese cultural influence through Korea. After 607, a whole host of influences were suddenly accessible to the Japanese people through their contact with China. When the first Japanese ambassador to China arrived in Ji, the Chinese capital, in 607, he would have seen vast lake-and-island gardens, encircled by pavilions, surrounding the imperial palaces. China must have been a revelation to the Japanese, and this was the beginning of many centuries of cultural exchange.

Above: *The gardens of Tenryu-ji are situated in Kyoto. Created in the 1300s, some parts were later adapted to fit with changing tastes.*

THE CHINESE STYLE

In Chinese gardens, islands were often used to represent the Mystic Isles, the mythical abode of the immortals. The Chinese Emperor Han Wu had built his own lake and a fantastical island garden in the hope of enticing the immortals down to part with the secret elixir for eternal youth. The Mystic Isles were believed to float on the backs of turtles, while the immortals were carried around on the backs of cranes. These myths had a huge impact on the Japanese imagination and, to this day, the Mystic Isles, cranes and turtles still feature prominently, usually in the form of carefully composed rock groupings. Rocks not only represented islands, however, but also came to symbolize Mount Shimusen, the central mountain in Buddhist mythology and an important mountain-water image that arrived in Japan from China.

BUDDHIST INFLUENCE

A major force in Japan, Buddhism gained particular importance from the mid-6th century onwards, incorporating additional Chinese influences. Even though the emperor of Japan placed the country under the protection of the Buddha, the indigenous Shinto gods, or kami, retained a strong influence, closely associated with the emperor and with the general well-being of society.

Ponds were central to the Buddhist concept of paradise and became as essential to Japanese gardens as they had been in China. The Amida Buddha's Land of Paradise garden was described as being planted with gem-laden trees, while golden sands edged lily-filled lakes. On these lakes, heavenly hosts waited for devout souls to give them new birth on a lotus blossom in the realm of bliss. The great Amida garden of lakes and islands became the image for Nara- and Heian-style gardens.

THE ONSET OF THE JAPANESE STYLE

In 794, when the capital was moved to what is now Kyoto (Heian Kyo), the pond-and-winding-stream garden was the pre-eminent garden design.

Left: *Ancient Chinese gardens displayed trees and fantastic rocks in their courtyards. The Japanese, although heavily influenced by the Chinese, had a preference for a more naturalistic approach to garden design.*

Above: *The Chinese myths of the Mystic Isles still inspire designers today. In the dry garden of Ryogen-in, created in the 1980s, stands the central mountainous island of Horai.*

Left: *A landscape of mountains and a river by Japanese painter and Zen priest Toya Sesshu (1420–1506). His Zen-inspired landscapes were influential within both the painting and garden design styles of Japan.*

Gradually, during the Heian period, fuelled by the cultured society of Kyoto, a true Japanese garden style began to emerge. This style slowly and indiscernibly blended Buddhism, the Mystic Isles and Shinto's sacred groves into the distinctive art form that is so recognizable today.

GEOMANCY

Meaning the Chinese science of divination, geomancy affected the design of palaces, towns and gardens by its insistence that buildings, plants and rocks must be placed in a very precise manner according to certain forces or lines of energy, to ensure that they were in balance and in tune with the natural order. If a placement was wrong, trouble and ill health could descend on an individual, a whole household or even the nation. In fact, the choice of the site of the new city of

Kyoto, modelled on the Chinese city of Chang'an and its palaces and gardens, followed Chinese geomantic principles.

Each of the elements is linked to a direction: earth at the centre, water in the north, fire to the south, wood in the east and metal in the west. Other Chinese approaches to the elements maintained that each direction could also represent colours, planets, seasons and guardian gods.

The principles of yin and yang also form part of the science of geomancy, but they are not always regarded as precise opposites and may be seen as complementary forces. Most phenomena contain an element of both yin and yang, because bringing them together produces harmonious conditions. For example, combining water (yin) with the sun or fire (yang) creates the right conditions to enable seeds to germinate.

Above: *A turtle island at Konchi-in where the head and flippers can be picked out from among rocks and clipped shrubs.*

PAINTINGS

The next wave of influences on the Japanese garden also came from China, in part through its painters. The Chinese artists of the Tang and Song dynasties painted mountains, pine trees beside waterfalls, streams falling into lakes, and paths weaving through rocks. These artists, more than all of the great Chinese imperial parks, influenced the Japanese garden. Meanwhile, Japanese monks and artists who visited China saw temples of great beauty, as well as hermit monks and artists living a simple life in huts and caves, and they returned home with a desire to emulate the Chinese lifestyle and the arts that they had encountered there.

ZEN BUDDHISM

Japanese monks were eager to practise a purer version of Buddhism without esoteric practices such as the worship of Buddha Amida. They found in China practitioners of Chan (or Zen, as it is known in Japan), a word derived from the Sanskrit *dyana*, which means meditation. Zen Buddhism places much more focus on the individual and on his or her efforts to control the mind, especially through meditation, and the experience of "no-ness".

By the late 1500s, Japanese Zen masters had become the next great garden-makers, once again inspired by Chinese and Japanese paintings featuring dry gardens of sand and rocks. Their gardens became increasingly abstract, often carrying hidden messages of Zen symbolism.

TEA GARDENS AND CEREMONIES

The paintings, poetry and spiritual writings of the Chinese literati were not the only sources of inspiration for Japanese painters and Zen monks. The design of the Japanese tea house was also inspired by the rustic hermitages of the Chinese literati and artists residing in their mountain retreats. As a result, the merchants and monks would develop a completely new style of garden, which included a path (known as a *roji*) that led to a tea house.

By the early 16th century, this new style had evolved into the influential form of the tea garden, and Japanese garden design took a brand new imaginative direction. The Japanese tea garden is one that is very familiar to Western eyes, with its key features such as a tea house, lanterns, water basins and wells.

Top right: *This two-fold screen by Kano Eitoku (1543–90) shows a romantic depiction of birds and a waterfall.*

Right: *In the garden at Konchi-in, various symbolic forms are depicted with rocks and pines, with fine white gravel spread around them to represent the sea.*

Modern & Western influences

From 1633, when shogun Iemitsu declared the Japanese borders closed, until the Americans arrived to reopen them by force in 1852, Japan was a hidden, secret country. Very few links with the West survived during this period, and even the Chinese had little contact with their neighbours. While the country developed in isolation during the major part of the Edo period (1603–1867), Japanese artists continued to express themselves in painting, literature and design, making use of a strong internal cultural tradition in which artistic endeavour could flourish.

THE AMERICAN ATTACK

Until 1852, when the Black Ships of the American Navy fired their first few warning salvos at the Tokugawa shogunate to force the Japanese to open their ports and begin trading with foreigners, the influence of the modern Western world had been limited. Once these trading and communication channels opened, the West's influence made a mark in technical and artistic terms. This was a two-way interaction, as the impact of Japanese culture in the West was also significant.

The Japanese regime in 1852 was in a sad state of decline. However, after the American attack, the impoverished imperial family replaced the shogunate that had held power for 250 years, and enjoyed a new ascendancy.

Above: *The roof garden of the Canadian Embassy in Tokyo, designed by the Buddhist monk Shunmyo Masuno in the 1990s, and inspired by the Rocky Mountains.*

Below: *Mirei Shigemori, an artist and garden maker, redesigned the garden of Tofuku-ji in Kyoto, in the 1930s. He was the first to see the potential of the Japanese garden to become a vehicle for contemporary expression. He was also influenced by the Western art forms of the time.*

JAPANESE ARTS REACH THE WEST

From the mid-19th century onwards Japan's influence on the West made itself felt, with Japanese prints and artefacts flooding Western markets, invigorating the art world and inspiring the Impressionists, among others. Great architects, such as Frank Lloyd Wright (1869–1959) and Charles Rennie Mackintosh (1868–1928), found a raw simplicity in Japanese gardens and architecture. They also admired the beauty of natural materials, which they used in conjunction with their own modern materials: glass, concrete and steel.

In gardening terms, what particularly appealed to Western eyes was the style of extraordinary gardens such as the Ryoan-ji, in Kyoto, whose brooding mystery affects people as much now as it did when it was built in the 1490s. This Zen-style garden influenced many Western designers who, although perhaps unfamiliar with the concepts of Zen Buddhism, found in the garden an art form that gave expression to their own minimalist, atonal and avant-garde creations.

WESTERN ARTS REACH JAPAN

While the West was absorbing Eastern influences, the Japanese showed an extraordinary capacity to assimilate other traditions, both digesting and also reinventing them. There was (and still is), for example, a hunger for English-style gardens, which were initially copied, as Chinese gardens had been, before being integrated into the Japanese mainstream and given an Eastern slant.

MODERN JAPANESE DESIGN

By the 1930s, however, the design of more traditional Japanese gardens had become rather stale and clichéd, and this situation prompted one or two designers to re-evaluate the use of established materials and motifs. The greatest of these was Mirei Shigemori (1896–1975), who made private and temple gardens from the 1930s to the

1950s. He gave his gardens a modern twist but, interestingly, continued to employ traditional motifs and natural materials alongside the contemporary use of concrete.

Since the 1950s, many newly created gardens have replaced natural rocks and boulders with raw, blasted, quarried materials, plastics and metals, in much the same way as 17th-century gardens blended the artificial with the natural. This incorporation of new materials, while retaining the pure simplicity of Zen gardens, is still the hallmark of contemporary Japanese garden design.

One of the latest movements in the evolution of the Japanese garden is towards a more natural style of garden

Above: *A Japanese tea garden, designed by Maureen Busby for the 2004 RHS Chelsea Flower Show in London. The main feature of a tea garden is a stepping-stone path that passes through a "wilderness".*

design, featuring a combination of both native plantings and naturalistic streams. However, what also stands out with these contemporary Japanese gardens is that Japan cannot entirely shed its cultural and historical past and that, even now, the most up-to-date garden designs still hark back through the ages to the 11th-century Heian gardens in their use of natural materials, as was laid down in the oldest surviving work on Japanese gardening – the *Sakuteiki*.

INSPIRATIONS

The Japanese garden possesses a style quite unlike any other. This unique character can be attributed to three factors: the outstanding natural landscape and the spirit of Zen, which both inspired it, and the importance of architectural features within the garden.

Japan is an archipelago of rugged coastlines and has a volcanic mountainous landscape, with steep rocky streams that tumble through forests. This wonderful natural topography and native flora inspired gardeners to recreate in their own gardens what they saw around them. The ancient Japanese also believed that the trees, rocks, mountains and water had power over the gods of their Shinto religion.

The pared-down, minimalist way of interpreting and recreating the natural landscape around them within the garden originated in the spirit of Zen, with the careful use of space and understatement.

A final factor to consider is the spiritual significance of architectural features in the Japanese garden, including the tea houses, and the technique of *shakkei*, whereby views both within and beyond the garden are framed by manmade or natural elements.

This chapter looks at the features that make the character of the Japanese garden distinct, and explains how this style can be understood and interpreted in the West.

Above: *Plum blossom is associated with the start of spring.*
Left: *In the garden of Hosen-in in the mountains north of Kyoto, a clipped hedge frames the natural landscape and draws it in through the stems of bamboo.*

The natural landscape

Looking out over an expanse of sand raked into perfect lines, set in a perfect rectangular courtyard with one or two rocks, and an azalea or two clipped so much that they barely flower, you might be forgiven for thinking that Japanese gardeners are more inclined to fly in the face of nature than sympathize with it. Yet Japan's own natural landscape of mountains, windswept pines, waterfalls and islands directly inspires and informs their garden designs, resulting in a spiritual style that gives inspiration to gardeners all over the world.

Above: *Under certain conditions, snow will stick to pine needles. In Japan these attractive white baubles are commonly known as "snow flowers".*

AN INSPIRING STYLE

Japanese garden design was initially influenced by the Chinese. However, the natural mountainous and coastal landscapes of Japan, coupled with the people's spiritual reverence for rocks and trees, derived from their native Shinto religion, together created a second powerful influence. By incorporating a careful selection of indigenous plants and imitating the natural features of the countryside, albeit in a restrained, stylized form, Japanese garden designers have developed a unique style.

THE TOPOGRAPHY OF JAPAN

A mountainous archipelago of four main islands, Japan also has hundreds of small rocky islets. The mountains – over 50 of which are volcanic – are steep and wooded and scored with rocky streams, hot springs and rivers. In fact, most are still wooded up to their peaks because, until recently, Buddhism was the official religion and the eating of meat and fish was prohibited. This meant that, unlike in other parts of the world, their hills and mountains have not been stripped of vegetation by sheep, goats and cattle. To this day, natural features such as mountains, rocks and streams continue to inspire Japanese garden designers and are recurring features of the Japanese garden.

THE MOUNTAIN MOTIF

Mountains are a uniquely powerful influence over the imagination and gardens of the Chinese and the Japanese. Through myth and religion, mountains stand as the central feature of many of their garden designs. The Mystic Isles myth (which developed off the Chinese coast) is a typical example. There were five islands, one of which was called P'eng-lai, which later became Horai in Japan. These Mystic Isles, like the real islands of Japan, were large and mountainous, towering thousands of feet high, their sides steep and precipitous, reaching up to high plateaux rich in greenery. Here were misty blue valleys where all the beasts and birds were white, trees bore pearls, the flowers were fragrant and the fruits brought immortality to those who ate them. Along the shores of the islands lived blissfully happy immortal beings in golden, silver and jade pleasure pavilions. The immortals were not gods, but men who suffered no sickness or death, and developed supernatural powers, being able to float through the air. Sometimes they were carried on the backs of giant cranes, another key feature of Japanese design.

Originally, the myth says, the Mystic Isles floated about and were not fixed to the ocean floor. Then, the Supreme Ruler of the Universe commanded the islands to be secured by 15 enormous turtles, but one day a giant cast a net and caught six of the turtles.

Right: *Vermilion Torii gates originate in Shinto religion and symbolize sacred ground. They make a bold feature in the Karlsruhe Japanese garden in Germany.*

SYMBOL OF SHINTO: THE *TORII* GATE

The typical vermilion-painted gateway to Shinto shrines may be found at the entrance to many Buddhist temples as well. The gateway marks the progress of the worshipper from the day-to-day world outside to the sacred world inside, and passing under it is part of the cleansing ritual common to Shinto and Buddhist worship. *Torii* gates are usually made of wood, metal or stone, with two upright supports and two crossbars over the top. The word *torii* is thought to derive from a resting perch for birds; the birds will bring good luck to the temple, as they are considered to be messengers from the gods in the Shinto religion. These days, wealthy visitors to a Shinto shrine may donate a new *Torii* gate to thank the gods for their success in business.

Some others drifted away and were lost, leaving just three. The early Japanese might well have believed that they already lived on these Mystic Isles. Whatever the case, the island of Horai, the crane and the turtle became themes embedded in their gardens, even being reproduced in Mirei Shigemori's garden at the Tofukuji, as recently as 1938.

When you add to this ancient myth the divinities of Shinto (see below), the natural landscape of Japan, the influence of the distantly revered and idealized landscapes of China, and the Lands of Paradise promised by some Buddhist sects, the whole concoction becomes an inspirational mix for the development of a very special and beautiful style of gardening.

THE INFLUENCE OF SHINTO

Shinto – the religion of Japanese settlers who arrived by sea, possibly from Korea, in the 3rd or 4th centuries – means "way of the gods". It involved animistic and pagan-style rituals, and centred around rocks,

Above: *Although boldly abstract, the design of the Site of Reversible Destiny in Gifu, Japan, incorporates the mountain motif while also echoing the form of the distant landscape.*

trees and plants. It was believed that these objects possessed spiritual aspects that could draw the gods down to earth. There were two kinds of gods, or *kami*: those that descended from above, and those that lived across the sea and gave birth to the main islands of Japan. These two sets of gods were symbolized by sacred rocks and sacred ponds. These rock and pond motifs occur again and again in Japanese gardens, both past and present.

The Shintoists believed that certain places in the wild were inhabited by

the gods. To this day, you will still find trees wrapped in ropes near shrines, as well as old trees and rocks that have become shrines in their own right. *Shime*, the binding of objects or even people with rice straw ropes, may originally have been used to designate territory, while the bound artefacts symbolize land or islands. It is interesting to note that the word *shima*, meaning "garden", comes from shime.

Go-shintai ("the home of the gods") and *iwa-kura* ("seats of the gods") can also still be found throughout Japan. They have been purified and covered with layers of sand and gravel to become *shiki-no-himorogi*, or "sacred precincts". Some special rocks may even have been added.

Such rituals and sacred spaces had an important influence on the use of rocks in gardens and dry landscape gardens. The interplay between the flat expanse of the sea (symbolized by sand or gravel) and the rugged immensity of rocks and old trees provided a kind of aesthetic that inspired the leap from the purely spiritual space of Shinto to the secular space of the garden. This aesthetic

Left: *Detail from a screen (c.1600–1640) illustrating episodes from* The Tale of Genji. *This classic of ancient Japanese literature is interwoven with symbolic references to nature.*

Right: *At the end of the 19th century, the designer Ogawa created gardens inspired by nature. This recalled the early gardens of the 10th century, such as this one at Syoko-ho-en, near Kyoto.*

may also explain why the Chinese style of garden was not copied "religiously". Shinto and the natural landscape of Japan provided a fertile influence that adapted the Chinese style into something new.

INTERPRETATIONS OF NATURE

The natural world has been a constant feature of Japanese gardens from the early days of the Heian period (794–1185), when inspiration came straight from the landscape and natural surroundings, right up to the present, when abstract and contemporary gardens still demonstrate a profound understanding of nature. The Italian garden aims to express an intellectual and philosophical vision of nature; the English garden is mainly based on the idealized world of the pastoral idyll; but the Japanese garden uses nature in a highly symbolic way.

More specifically, in the 15th and 16th centuries, Japanese designers turned increasingly to their great landscape painters for artistic inspiration, just as the late 18th-century English picturesque garden was inspired by the paintings of Claude Lorrain and Nicolas Poussin. Along with nature, painting has been a common starting point for many gardening movements.

THE *SAKUTEIKI*

The earliest known treatise on gardening, the *Sakuteiki* – the subtitle of which was "Setting of Stones" – was written in the mid-11th century. It was more of a technical journal for the select few, but many of its rules are still adhered to today as elemental precepts. Stones are said to have "desires", and the book recommends ways of listening to them, vital if they are to be placed correctly in the Japanese garden, as if they were in the wild.

The chapter headed "Nature" describes the remarkable and vivid use of the imagery of coastlines, streams, rocks, islands and waterfalls in garden design, and details a range of features with specific instructions. For example, stones can be used in different ways – perhaps placed in streams in order to modulate the flow of water, used as bottom or solitary stones, or as diffused stones to interrupt and divert the flow. Furthermore, garden streams (*yarimizu*) can be created in various styles, for example as if they are flowing through a valley, or as if they are broad rivers, or mountain torrents. There are also descriptions of, and instructions for creating, different kinds of waterfall, all of which are relevant to the Japanese gardener today.

Garden streams often pour down a waterfall into a lake or pond. These ponds represent lakes or the sea, and are dotted with islands, their shorelines punctuated by promontories made of white sand to evoke the beaches of distant landscapes. Miniature windswept ocean beaches, coves and undulating shorelines are planted with soft grasses. Islands also come in different guises, with rocky shores, for example, or in forest, meadow and wetland styles.

The earliest Japanese gardens, from the Heian period when the *Sakuteiki* was written, still have an important influence on modern garden designers who look to nature for inspiration. These gardens emphasize that we should observe but not slavishly copy nature, consulting the "genius of the place" before transforming it into art. As the *Sakuteiki* suggests, "Visualize the famous landscapes of our country and come to understand their most interesting points. Recreate the essence of these scenes in the garden, but do so interpretatively, not strictly."

HEIAN CULTURE AND DESIGN

In the culture of the Heian period, as distinct from the later austere Zen and Muromachi periods, the aristocracy that had settled around the Emperor in Kyoto enjoyed years of peaceful luxury. They spent much of their time writing poetry, and became more and more detached from the business of running the country. A kind of melancholy pervaded their lives. They believed that they were living in the *Mappo*, the Buddha's period of Ending Law, with declining social and religious mores. They hoped to be transported to his Western Paradise, depicted in their gardens as lakes and islands, for an afterlife of eternal bliss. This life was seen as a fleeting interlude, a dream between two realities.

The Heian aristocracy closely observed nature, noting every whim and expression as a sign and symbol to compare with love, death, honour and the great range of human emotions. These emotions were often symbolized by plants, and the early Heian gardens used many flowering shrubs, such as kerria, deutzia, lespedeza, azalea and osmanthus, as well as cherries, maples, wild roses and irises. In the two great novels of the time, *The Pillow Book* (995) by Sei Shonagon and *The Tale of Genji* (early 11th century) by Murasaki Shikibu, trees and flowers, as well as the weather, were used to symbolize human thoughts and desires.

THE SEASONS AND THEIR PLANTS

Around Kyoto, the seasons are fairly predictable, right down to the first rumblings of thunder over the mountains that herald the beginning of the rainy season in midsummer. By then, the cherry blossom, wisteria and azalea will have long dropped their last blooms and the hydrangeas started to colour. At the same time, it will be sweltering in the sub-tropical south in Kyushu, while in northern Honshu and Hokkaido, trees growing below the melting snows on the mountainsides have not yet come into

Top: *The cherry blossom heralds the height of spring and is the most popular season for viewing gardens in Japan.*

Above: *The mop-headed* Hydrangea macrophylla, *growing profusely in a shaded woodland, is a classic summer flower.*

leaf. Apart from the northern reaches, most of Japan endures uncomfortably hot and rainy summers. This is why the Heian elite in Kyoto placed such a strong emphasis on the two main garden seasons – spring (the most important) and autumn – an emphasis that still exists today. The seasons

were also considered to be part of the geomantic system, with flowers used to depict the cardinal lines of energy; good planting and design helped to protect the household from misfortune.

In modern Japan, the plum and peach blossoms are the fanfare for spring, followed shortly by the cherry blossom.

Top: *Trees are planted extensively in Japanese gardens for their autumn colour, such as this katsura tree in the Tully garden in Ireland.*

Above: *The vivid colour of a traditional Japanese* Torii *gate stands out dramatically in a snow-covered garden.*

Then come the native camellias, azaleas and floribunda wisterias, while, in early summer, iris festivals are celebrated up and down the country. The lotus, the enduring symbol of Buddhism, also flowers in summer. The autumn is marked by the Japanese maples (*Acer palmatum*) which grow in Japan's forests, as does *Enkianthus*, which sets ablaze the hillsides and hillside temples at this time. Chrysanthemums, symbols of the imperial family, long life and good fortune, are grown especially for festivals in late autumn. In winter, the pine, cedar and bamboo are celebrated.

The Japanese use some native plants, such as cherries, azaleas, pines and bamboos, within their gardens, but tend to ignore a vast range of their native flora. This indicates restraint rather than a limited palette. So a hedge may be made up of a number of evergreen shrubs but will not blend masses of bright-coloured foliage. In this way, the final effect is restrained even when a large number of plants have been used.

The influence of Zen

Zen Buddhism was introduced to Japan from China by monks in the 13th century. Once established, it provided a consistent influence for all aspects of Japanese culture and arts. The "no-ness" of Zen philosophy, in particular, prompted some important developments in garden design – the dry gardens surrounding many Buddhist temples were a rich source of inspiration for Japanese garden designers and the influence of this simple, restrained style, with its symbolic use of raked effects in gravel and the subtle placing of rocks, has been felt from East to West.

Above: *Natural rocks have been replaced by slabs of blasted quarry stone and assembled with fragments of the rock. The mountain image and empty space are typical features of the Zen garden.*

THE ARRIVAL OF ZEN BUDDHISM

The pioneer monks who introduced Zen to Japan initially met with a bleak response from the rather philistine military government based in Kamakura, south of present-day Kyoto. Two or three generations later, however, Zen found new patrons among the rival warlords and the imperial family so that, by the early 1300s, there were some 300 Zen monasteries in Kamakura and Kyoto. These temples, part of what was called the Five Mountain Network, promoted studies in a range of Chinese arts and philosophies. Apart from studying neo-Confucian metaphysics, the monks were also highly skilled in poetry, painting, calligraphy, ceramics, architecture and garden design.

A less erudite group of rural monks, who were known as Rinka (meaning "forest"), practised in another network of Zen temples and devoted themselves strictly to Zazen, or sitting Zen (meditation), as well as *koan* (the writing of riddles). Their self-discipline and loyalty to their masters appealed to the rising warrior class, the samurai, to whom the Rinka monks preached stern moralizing sermons. This philosophy was shared by other followers of Zen, whose teachers or masters also transmitted their values to their disciples. There were no written scriptures, though, and none of the trappings of esoteric Buddhism, such as mandalas, chanting and the reciting of scriptures, which had dominated Japanese life for the previous 500 years.

ZEN AND THE DRY GARDEN

Dogan (1200–53), a monk who lived during the Kamakura period, was well known for emphasizing the "no-ness" of all things (emptiness, void or non-substantiality). This aspect of Zen meant finding what might be called the "perfect expression of pure mind". Garden designers expressed this "no-ness" in the empty space of sand in dry gardens. Sand had already been used within Shinto sacred precincts, then in front of palaces for court

Left: *The stump of an enormous Japanese cedar bound and housed as a shrine in its own right. The Shinto belief that trees, rocks and other natural objects possessed spirits was incorporated into Zen garden design.*

Above: *Rocks in a "sea" of gravel represent the Mystic Isles, from the ancient myth adopted by the Zen tradition.*

Right: *Zen monks were drawn to the world of the Chinese scholar-hermit. They created tea houses, such as this one at Toji-in Temple, and tea paths imbued with the spirit of Zen.*

ceremonies, before evolving into a representation of the sea or a white canvas for painter-gardeners. Under the auspices of Zen practitioners, the empty stretch of sand came to represent a meditative spiritual space. Sometimes these gardens look like familiar landscapes, or brush paintings, and if contemplated for long enough, they induce a sense of calm.

It was mostly the Zen monks who designed the extraordinary spaces known as *kare-sansui* (dry landscapes), which have become synonymous with Japanese gardening, most notably at the famous dry gardens of Ryoan-ji and Daisen-in. Zen exercised a strong influence over Japanese gardening (and still does), and it also gave greater precision and discipline to the art of garden design. Even if you are not steeped in the mysteries of Zen, you can appreciate the extraordinary beauty and sense of style and the pared-down, abstract visions of nature to be found in these gardens.

Right: *At the Canadian embassy in Tokyo, a dry garden with natural rocks and sand pays homage to the past while also displaying the brave cutting edge of modernity.*

ZEN AND THE TEA GARDEN

The evolution of the tea garden had strong links to the Zen monks. Used originally by them as an aid to wakefulness during long periods of meditation, tea soon became an essential part of Buddhist rituals. It was only a short step for Zen monks, as garden makers and tea drinkers, to bring these two arts together. So the tea garden, at first just a simple rustic path to the tea house, became associated with important traditions.

ZEN AND MODERN GARDEN STYLE

When creating a Zen-style dry garden, consider the influences that created them. Many contemporary gardens are made up of a few rocks, a layer of sand or gravel and a bamboo plant or pine tree, and are glibly described as being very Japanese or, worse, very Zen. That is only true, however, if there is no hint of the superfluous. Nor should any one feature dominate. Zen-style dry gardens, or tea gardens, should be imbued with purity and restraint.

THE ESSENCE OF THE ZEN GARDEN

While the first Japanese gardens of the 11th century were poetic readings of nature and 15th-century gardens were inspired readings of the master landscape painters, the gardens of both periods were disciplined attempts to understand the self and the universe. What this meant in practical terms was that there was an avoidance of the trite, the obvious and the emphatic. Unnecessary distractions and the use of excessive colour or form were also avoided. The prime ingredients were those that in the 13th century became defined as the seven aspects of Zen:

• asymmetry
• simplicity
• austere sublimity
• naturalness
• tranquillity
• subtle profundity
• freedom from attachment

These qualities were also applied to other art forms in a Zen style, such as calligraphy and poetry.

Even people with no experience of meditation or of Zen Buddhism can appreciate the calming beauty of a Zen garden. If you want to imbue your garden with the spirit of Zen, you should try to make your garden reflect a quiet, contemplative world and avoid the kind of deliberate gestures that come from a busy, overactive mind. The art is to avoid over-stimulating the senses in the way that you might experience in a Western garden.

A Zen garden will avoid carefully contrived colour schemes, rocks with strange shapes, gushing fountains or brightly painted buildings. For example, the red-painted Chinese bridges that you see in some Japanese gardens would not be seen in a Zen garden because such features were

Above: *The Zen garden of Tenju-an, in Kyoto, dating from the late 14th century, is a superb example of the interplay between geometric, manmade and irregular natural forms.*

seen to divert the eye and stimulate the mind instead of calming it.

It is the approach to the Zen arts that is important, whether it be in garden design, painting or the martial arts. The spirit of Zen, the "emptiness" conveyed by an area of raked gravel in a dry garden, should be as much in the mind of the man with the rake as in the clean sweep of the gravel. Although Zen is a state of mind that takes years to perfect, the garden designer can still plan a garden with the spirit of Zen in mind, making calmness and tranquillity a central feature, avoiding bright colours and ensuring that the landscaping and planting are kept to an absolute minimum.

Zen garden with raked waves

This dry garden in Ryongen-in, Kyoto, was redesigned and constructed in 1980 on the site of an old garden. The "canvas" of this painterly garden is a rectangle of a sea with parallel raked waves. Maintained in a more exaggerated form than older gardens of this style, the essential elements are the same as those of the 15th century. The parallel lines of raked gravel change to deep concentric waves as they lap around the main features in the dry sea. Towards the back is the tallest group of rocks, which represent Mount Horai (*Horai-san*), the foremost of the Mystic Isles. These isles were said to be carried on the backs of turtles, so the main mossy island is designed as a turtle island (*kame-shima*). The immortals lived on these isles, holding the secret elixir for eternal youth and immortality. They travelled around on the backs of cranes, and the third rock arrangement is a crane island (*tsuru-shima*).

The rectangular frame is made from a combination of edging stones and roof tiles. On two sides a border of moss is contained between the edging and the wall, while in the foreground the temple veranda and garden are divided by a border of pebbles. Pine trees have also been planted into the border.

The garden can be read as an artistic impression, with the bolder shapes and the deeper waves creating a dramatic effect on the viewer. Nevertheless, the simplicity of the design and the significance of the main features give a sense of permanence.

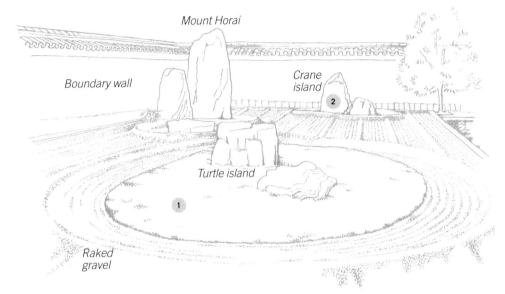

Mount Horai

Boundary wall

Crane island

Turtle island

Raked gravel

Right: *In the dry garden at Ryogen-in, the three main symbols of the Mystic Isles are laid out in a sea of sand. In the foreground is a turtle island; back left is Mount Horai, the tallest of the Mystic Isles; with a crane island at the rear.*

Architectural elements

Up to the Edo period (1603–1867), all major garden styles evolved in towns and were defined by the layout of the main buildings, courtyards, entrances and boundaries. Later, large gardens were laid out in more rural locations, where small buildings such as arbours, pavilions and tea houses were often placed to keep the human focus, so maintaining the relationship between architecture and garden. Another role for architecture was in the technique of *shakkei*, where buildings, trees or shrubs would frame a view of the landscape beyond the garden.

ARCHITECTURAL INTERACTION

The relationship between a Japanese garden and the architecture of the main house, temple or garden buildings is quite unlike that of the formal Western garden. In the West, the details and forms of the architecture tend to influence the design of formal gardens, but by contrast the formal Japanese garden enjoys the interplay between the angularity of the architecture and the curve of natural forms. Although dry and courtyard gardens are often contained within the rectilinear confines of garden walls, the forms of the gardens themselves are more like paintings held within a picture frame.

Above: *In the dry garden at the Tofuku-ji, the architectural line of the* hojo *abbot's quarters, the surrounding walls and the lines of raked sand make it hard to define exactly where the building ends and the garden begins.*

Below: *The view from the temple veranda overlooking the garden at Shoden-ji reveals not only the garden but also the distant sacred Mount Hiei. This capturing of a view was part of the garden design device known as* shakkei.

This contemporary design by Maureen Busby shows a strong interplay between the buildings and the gardens that surround them.

In other styles of Japanese garden, the natural forms of stepping stones, rocks, pine boughs and bamboos are brought very close to the buildings. Sometimes camellias or azaleas may be clipped into geometric forms to accentuate or even imitate the architecture, but asymmetry and dynamic natural forms within the design are usually preferred.

CHINESE INFLUENCES

The Japanese buildings of the Nara (710–94) and Heian (794–1185) periods, like their gardens, were more or less copies of the Chinese. But differences began to develop during the Heian period: the Japanese already showed a preference for the natural finish of timber, rather than the more flamboyant painted buildings common in China at the time, and roofs were also less sweeping and curved than their Chinese counterparts.

GARDEN BUILDINGS

Japanese garden buildings and structures have particular characteristics that mark them as different from most Western styles:

• the preferred materials are natural, such as bamboo, reed, and sawn or raw timber (sometimes with the bark on);

• materials are not painted, but left to look as natural as possible;

• at times when the Chinese influence was strong, especially the very early Nara period (early 8th century) and the later Edo period (early- to mid-19th century), buildings and structures, such as bridges, were sometimes painted bright red-orange, in dramatic contrast to the typically muted look apparent in the rest of the garden.

The principal style of Heian aristocratic homes was known as *shinden* (literally, "sleeping hall"). This main hall, or *shinden*, was set at the centre of a square building, with two adjacent wings to the sides for concubines and wives. From these two wings, two corridors (the east and the west) led south to the main garden. In the space between these two corridors was an open, sand-covered courtyard, which was reserved for ceremonies and entertainment. Through part of this courtyard, a stream might meander and feed into the main pond beyond.

At the end of the east and west corridors were pavilions, usually named after their primary function – for instance, the fishing pavilion was often built on stilts over the main pond, but was just as likely to have been used by musicians. Another pavilion may have covered the well or the spring that fed the pond.

Over the next 200 years, Japanese architecture evolved into smaller and more refined urban residences. By the Muromachi period, monks and samurai showed a marked preference for the *shoin* style. *Shoin* was a term that referred to the alcove that was set within one of the outer walls of the main building. This alcove had papered walls in order to allow natural light to illuminate a specially designed shelf or a desk for reading and writing. The *shoin* was a kind of library or study that, for the warriors and abbots, symbolized their arrival as members of the intelligentsia or literati. This new architectural style was found in many temples and houses, which also had verandas and sliding panels that opened up to reveal their gardens.

The tea house also employed some aspects of the *shoin* style, especially the alcove, but the general style of tea-house architecture was more rustic. The Japanese tea house, which was originally known as the "mountain place in the city", combined the rustic charm of the thatched hut (*soan*) with the sophistication of a more literary and urban style of architecture (*shoin*). This hybrid style was, and still is, most popular for building tea houses and garden buildings.

The alcove of the tea house, known as the *tokonoma*, was a place in which to display works of art, especially calligraphy scrolls and poems, alongside simple country-style flower arrangements.

SHAKKEI

Many old houses and temples have verandas with pillars that support the roofs. These pillars also frame a view of the garden. The view of the garden from indoors can be regarded as if you are looking at a painting. The art of framing is even more important when a spectacular distant view can be captured – for example, the sight of Mount Fuji, near Tokyo, or Mount Hiei, near Kyoto. This technique is called *shakkei*, or "borrowed scenery", but was once known by the more evocative term *ikedori*, meaning "captured alive". It was an important device that involved more than simply having a "nice view" from your house. *Shakkei* meant that prominent distant features could, in effect, be drawn into the garden itself and so become an intrinsic part of its overall composition.

Although most Westerners wishing to reproduce a Japanese garden will not own a Japanese-style home, they may have verandas, picture windows or other forms of framing that can be used to capture their garden, and perhaps also a more distant view. In this way, architecture can be used to make the garden part of the house.

Above: *The pillars that support the verandas of temples and tea houses can frame the garden beyond them in the same way as the frame of a landscape painting. This design accentuates the contrast between the architecture and the natural form.*

Below: *Sliding rice paper panel doors (*shoji*) open up a view from a tatami-matted tea room at Isui-en, Nara. The square opening interacts with the weaving stems of Japanese maples.*

FRAMING THE VIEW

If you are creating a Japanese garden around a Western-style house, think of how a Japanese house would interface with the garden. You should aim to:

• create key viewing points, where the garden and the distant view are framed as a complete composition;

• use large picture windows to frame the view of the garden and beyond;

• use the supporting pillars of a veranda or an arbour to frame a focal point;

• take extra care to frame the view of a dry garden.

Toji-in tea houses

Yoshimasa, the shogun of the late 15th century who inspired a great flowering of the arts of Japan, is said to have designed this thatched tea house in the garden of Toji-in. The garden is unusual in that it has two tea houses set side by side, and this helps to illustrate the design principles of the tea house. The style is derived from a combination of an older style of *shoin* architecture, including sliding panels, rice paper windows and a place to study, with the *soan* style of rustic huts of mountain farmers. The thatched roof is constructed in the same way as a farmer's house or barn, often including ventilation for silk worms, which were kept in the attic space. The rustic charm alludes to the Taoist hermit monks who lived in such buildings.

Traditional tea houses such as this often combine raw materials. Pillars made from tree trunks with the bark still on might feature, alongside strips of split bamboo and screens of natural plaster. There might also be finely carved shelves and surrounds to the *tokonoma*, the alcove inside the tea house where decorative objects were placed as a focus for the tea ceremony. The floor is laid out with tatami reed mats around a hearth set in the floor to heat the hot water for tea. While simple and appearing to be rustic, tea houses can be quite complicated and elaborate. The Toji-in tea house commands a view over the garden, but tea houses can also be placed in more secluded spots within a garden.

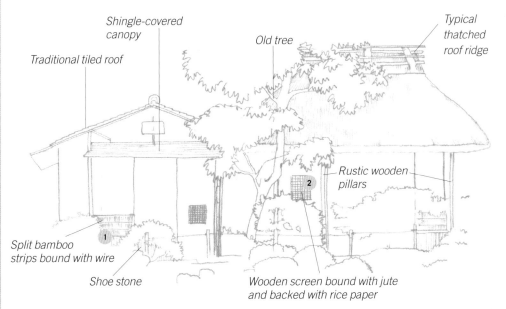

Shingle-covered canopy

Traditional tiled roof

Old tree

Typical thatched roof ridge

Rustic wooden pillars

Split bamboo strips bound with wire

Shoe stone

Wooden screen bound with jute and backed with rice paper

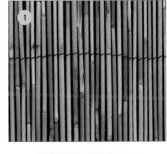

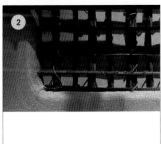

Right: *Two hermitage-style tea houses, built using contrasting materials, are set side by side in the gardens of Tojo-in, Kyoto. The simple architecture and thatched roof are modelled on those of rustic farm buildings.*

Understanding the Japanese garden

Despite the complexity of different kinds of Japanese garden, the common Western impression is of a small, carefully cultivated, stylized space, filled with clipped shrubs, rocks and stone artefacts such as lanterns, pagodas and Buddhas. In reality, the finest Japanese gardens are larger than many Western city gardens, and the artefacts are quite superfluous to their design. What counts is the spirit of the garden, and how the different elements are balanced. A sensitively styled Japanese garden should include the following principles.

NATURE AND RELIGIOUS SPIRIT

The beauty of many of the great Japanese gardens lies in their sublime vision of nature. The pleasure people took in the poetic beauty of flowers and cherry blossom that was so evident in the 11th century still lingers on in the celebratory cherry blossom festivals of today. The Japanese also held great reverence for their landscape gods and recognized the power of *yugen* ("hidden depth"), describing the feeling of awe that nature can evoke. This reverence has always been an important influence in the garden designs of Japan, inspiring the recreation of, for example, an open ocean, the way a river flows, and how a mountain range is encircled by mist.

ROCKS AND WATER

The standard elements of rocks and water are designed and placed to imitate as far as possible the way they occur in the natural landscape. So ponds should be created with naturalistic outlines, with inlets and gravel beaches just as if nature had shaped them. Rocks should not be positioned as individual, monolithic pieces, as they are in Chinese gardens, or admired in isolation as one would a piece of sculpture on a pedestal. They are also presented as part of the natural landscape.

NATURAL AND MANMADE ELEMENTS

Although water and rocks are the foundation of the garden, the design of any artefacts and buildings follows a carefully observed and orchestrated relationship between the natural and the manmade. The finely polished wooden panels of the tea house might be in-filled with rough plaster, while the wooden support posts might still have their bark on. The concept of *wabi-sabi* is equally important. This was a poetic term adopted by the tea masters to describe a quality of raw simple beauty, touched with the patina of age.

Above: *Monochromatic ink paintings with their simple brushwork were frequently imitated by the creators of Zen dry gardens.*

ASSYMMETRY AND BALANCE

Symmetry is rarely found in Japanese gardens, where the elements are characteristically arranged in odd numbers to bring to mind the asymmetry that characterizes nature.

Below: *The flat expanse of gravel, the horizontal lines of the hedge and some of the rocks in the Karlsruhe Japanese garden are balanced by several vertical rocks and the distant torii gate.*

Right: *There is no symmetry to this view, but all the elements are perfectly balanced. The large pond, crossed by a stepping-stone path, leads the eye to the trees, and the background is crowned by the Great Buddha Temple of Nara.*

Occasionally, an entranceway will have straight paths bordered by a pair of hedges or a view might be framed by rugged pine trees, but symmetry is generally seen by Japanese gardeners as something that restricts the imagination.

Instead of a symmetrical format, you need to create a design that feels natural, yet has a balanced composition, as well as a good sense of proportion between open and enclosed areas, enough empty space to allow the imagination to roam, and an easy transition from one section of the garden to another. The need for free-flowing movement applies not only to the observer's passage from area to area but also to specific elements. So paths and streams must meander and wander as they do in the wild, and ponds must appear to have naturally formed outlines.

ADDITIONAL NATURAL FEATURES

It can be useful to adopt the approach of the master painters when planning a Japanese garden, starting by dividing the site up into different layers:

• the foreground can be sand, gravel, moss or grass, featuring a water basin, rock or plant;

• the middle section can include a pond, island groups of rocks, and a weathered pine tree or clipped shrub;

• in the background, leave more open space with just the occasional rock, and use any distant view;

• frame the garden with an informal band of evergreens, walls or bamboo fencing.

CREATING LAYERS OF INTEREST

In the past, Japanese garden designers were inspired by old Japanese paintings. Composed with layers of interest and the artful play of light and shade, they helped them create a landscape's essence, framing it and dividing it into foreground, middle and distance.

Every element of a Japanese garden is there as part of the whole, whether a beautiful cherry tree or a millstone placed on a stepping-stone path.

Below: *The warm effect of the azaleas in this garden in Ito Shizuoka, Japan, shows how to integrate colour sensitively within the landscape.*

THE IMPORTANCE OF COLOUR

Although all the elements in a Japanese garden are subservient to the whole, this does not mean that the bright beauty of plum or cherry blossom or the autumn leaves of a maple are harmful to the design; they should be carefully considered for the part they play in celebrating the seasons. At the same time, plant colours should never be allowed to overwhelm a design, so showy, variegated, gold or purple foliage plants should in general be excluded. A good guide is that Japanese maples provide colour in the autumn and azaleas in the spring.

Interpreting a garden

The garden around the temple of Raikyu-ji, in Takahashi, was created by the 17th-century master gardener and tea-master Kobori Enshu. The central island set in a sea of gravel symbolizes Mount Horai and the Mystic Isles, and is wrapped in artistically clipped azaleas. The rounded shapes of the clipped shrubs that hug the main island emphasize the forms around them, either the rocks or the hilly landscapes that lie outside the garden. The effect is highly abstract, quite playful but also very sophisticated.

Each layer of the garden builds on the one before it. The foreground of raked sand, the rocks, the rolling "hills" of azaleas, the background evergreens, the spreading canopies of maples, all build up to the outline of Mount Atago in the distance.

Although essentially asymmetrical, this garden could be considered as very formal, and requires careful maintenance. The topiary, especially, needs a trained eye and a skilled hand to keep the shapes uniform. Each aspect of the design needs to be considered as part of the whole.

Also included are elements of the tea garden. A stepping-stone path starts at the temple and curls across the sea of gravel, behind the Mystic Isles and on around the garden into the shady depths of the trees. Here, a lantern has been carefully placed to light the path and to form another part of the overall composition.

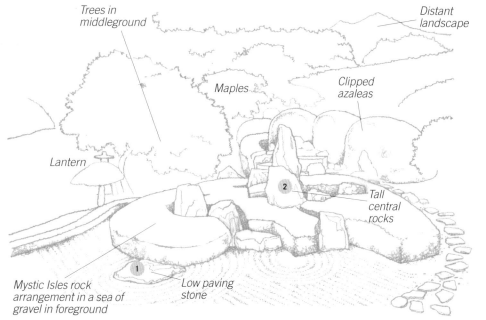

Trees in middleground

Distant landscape

Maples

Clipped azaleas

Lantern

2 — Tall central rocks

1

Mystic Isles rock arrangement in a sea of gravel in foreground

Low paving stone

1

2

Right: *The garden of Raikyu-ji, one of the masterpieces of Kobori Enshu (1579–1647). The gardens of this designer incorporate many of the essential elements of Japanese gardens in an elegant and balanced manner.*

Translating the style

Garden design in Japan is an ancient art form, and therefore one that is in tune with the country's culture and history. Indeed, Japanese gardens have often inspired other historic Japanese artworks, such as paintings on silk or parchment, porcelain decoration and poetry. The classic heritage of this gardening style is still preserved and valued within Japan and beyond, but it is also open to modern adaptation. There follows an evaluation of 19th- and 20th-century interpretations, and the challenges of using this established style and its traditional elements within modern gardens.

Above: *Although cobbles are often carefully set to imitate the flow of water, in this garden they have been placed with an emphasis that produces a more artistic effect.*

EARLY INTERPRETATIONS

When European and American gardeners became exposed to Japanese gardens in the late 1800s, most of them were only able to "read" them in the context of their own culture or of contemporary Japanese fashions. Japan had by then lost touch with its garden history. Zen was not properly understood at this stage, and it was only in the late 20th century that the true heart of the Japanese garden began to be more accurately interpreted.

Those early imitations of Japanese gardens created by Western gardeners in the late 19th and early 20th centuries included many of the artefacts found in authentic Japanese gardens, such as lanterns and pagodas, but these tended to be placed around ponds that were surrounded by the lush plantings so popular in Europe at the time. Many English "Japanese-style" gardens of this time were quite beautiful, with their blossoming rhododendrons and magnolias, but they were far from authentically Japanese.

These gardens are important for the way in which they illustrate the style of the times in which they were made, with the Japanese Garden at Tatton Park in Cheshire perhaps the best example. While English Victorian and Edwardian gardens in the Japanese style can be appreciated for their own beauty, their creators had little understanding of the principles behind Japanese garden design, and they should not be used as models by those wishing to follow in the Japanese tradition.

MINIMALISM AND ARTISTRY

As an abstract concept, the Japanese garden has become a springboard for modern designers. Minimalist gardens claim to owe much of their inspiration to Zen and its philosophy of "nothingness". While this may be partly true, these gardens often fail to capture the essence of a Japanese Zen garden. They tend to rely on manmade rather than natural materials, and lack the fine sense of proportion and balance so essential to the spirit of the Japanese garden.

Left: *In the precincts of the Shinto shrine of Kamigano, Kyoto, sits this pair of sand cones. Pairs of cones in a sea of sand are also found in some Zen gardens, as symbols of purification.*

GARDEN MATERIALS

One of the problems facing those keen to make Japanese gardens can be finding the right materials. It can be quite tricky and sometimes very expensive to buy some of the exact materials that you might find in a genuine Japanese garden. Rocks of the best kind may not be available in your area, and transport costs may be prohibitive. So you might ask yourself whether rocks are an essential element to your design, and consider the possibility that clipped plants such as azaleas would achieve an acceptable alternative, albeit creating an altogether different result.

The same is true for gravel. The search for the perfect gravel for a dry garden, of the right colour, size and texture, may not always be successful, and if you do use very fine gravel or sand it will require regular and careful maintenance.

To solve this problem you need to ask yourself some basic questions. If you want to avoid the trouble of raking and re-raking the gravel on a regular basis, a more ordinary gravel would be satisfactory and you could then use a simpler design that is easier to maintain.

Below: *Mirei Shigemori was the first Japanese garden designer to break with traditional design. This dry garden dates from the mid-1900s.*

Above: *This contemporary garden in Tofuku-ji interprets traditional brushwood fencing and rock representations with great inventiveness.*

Certainly, the Japanese have used gravel and rocks to such a peak of artistry that any garden design with a spread of gravel and artfully placed rocks will have a clear Japanese influence.

Any style of garden created away from its natural context will require an interpretation that suits your local conditions, your local resources, your budget and the space available. These constraints may in fact help to focus your creativity and inspire you to design a Japanese garden that is truly individual.

MODERN INTERPRETATIONS

There are examples of Japanese-style gardens being built on rooftops, using lightweight but realistic fibreglass rocks, and where the classic profile of the Japanese pine tree has been carved in metal. Similarly, concrete, stainless steel and fibreglass have all been used in contemporary Japanese gardens and are quite acceptable as part of a modern garden scheme. This approach is a different interpretation of the traditional style, but the essence of the Japanese garden is still clearly evident.

In the André Citroën gardens in Paris, the French garden designer Gilles Clément created a riverbed garden using gravel and dwarf willows bordered by silver-leafed shrubs. As in a Japanese Zen design, the garden is framed in a rectangle. He also placed stepping stones in the gravel, but instead of random stone he used raised square wooden blocks to cross over the "dry water" of the riverbed. The design is inspired by Japan in the use of gravel, stepping stones and the rectangular frame, but the whole is no longer identifiable as Japanese. It has transformed into something entirely original and unique.

The dry garden, a model that the Gilles Clément garden in Paris translates with such imagination, is an accessible one to emulate. It can be small, requires a minimum of planting and the basic materials of gravel or sand and rocks. The tea garden, with its reflections of journeys taken along paths through mountain wildernesses, finally arriving at a hermitage, is a concept that is wide open to contemporary interpretation.

Traditionally, pond and stroll gardens contain many artefacts, such as lanterns and pagodas, and these can appear excessive to Western tastes. A modern interpretation could, however, use the principle of a garden based around a pond but achieve this in a minimalist way without artefacts. The courtyard garden has perhaps the greatest potential in a modern garden as it is so intrinsically part of city culture and needs only a small space. This style of garden corresponds as closely with city gardens today as when they evolved in the Edo period in Japan.

Below: *The Jardin Argenté at Parc André Citroën in Paris is a modern and original design vision that has the clear spirit of the Japanese garden at its heart.*

Above: *Japanese black pines in the Huntington Botanical Gardens have been pruned to give a windswept look and combined with a rugged scree and bold rocks.*

CLASSIC GARDEN STYLES

When you start to think about choosing one of the five main styles of Japanese garden design – pond gardens, dry gardens, tea gardens, stroll gardens or courtyard gardens – you should understand that these are an over-simplification of a much more complex art form. But these categories do provide a good initial approach, and having made your choice, you can then add elements from other styles.

The first consideration will be what style will suit your garden or site best. A pond garden will need a fairly large area of at least a quarter of a hectare (roughly half an acre). A dry garden can be laid out in a very small space but ideally a flat one. A tea garden is more of a lifestyle decision than one dependent on the size or quality of the site. Tea gardens while traditionally complex and led by rituals, can in practice be small or extensive; paths can be long or short, undulating or flat; while the tea house can be secluded or prominent. Stroll gardens generally need a fair amount of space and a reliable source of water; they are best on uneven sites, where small hills can be raised and paths can wander around them. Finally, a courtyard garden can be as small as a few square metres (yards). This overview of the traditional styles will help you make your choice before you start to design your garden.

Above: *This rock evokes a Chinese junk floating in a bay.*
Left: *Symmetrical layout contrasts with the natural forms of Japanese maples in the dry garden at Tenju-an, Kyoto.*

Pond gardens

Ponds, lakes and streams have always been central to the Japanese garden, instilling a sense of tranquillity, joy and calm. Water features, such as ponds and streams, always appear totally natural within the surrounding landscape, even if they are constructed artificially, and obvious manmade features, such as fountains, are avoided. You do not need a particularly large garden to include an expanse of water, although the results will obviously be much more dramatic if you are able to construct a feature of some size and presence.

Above: *A turtle island carrying Mount Horai, from the myth of the Isles of the Immortals, in the Heian period garden of Motsu-ji.*

THE HISTORY OF POND GARDENS

There is a general nostalgia in Japan for a romantic period in Japan's history, exemplified by the stories in the *Tales of Genji* by Murasaki Shikibu. Although written in the 11th century, this is still a very popular novel. In it you will find references to many kinds of plants and to boating parties. Both in the 17th century, at the Katsura Palace, and in the 19th century, after the restoration of the emperor as the head of state, gardens were created to reawaken the spirit of those times. So although this style of garden is very old, it still has a place in the hearts of the Japanese today. The naturalistic aesthetic makes it all the more relevant in times when nature is so much under threat, especially in Japan.

THE POND GARDEN OF MOTSU-JI

We can gain some inspiration for the design of present-day pond gardens by looking briefly at a famous example from Japan's past, Motsu-ji, in Hiraizumi, Iwate, which is one of the very few surviving pond and island gardens from the 12th century. Today, you can still see Motsu-ji's great lake, which is bordered by formal iris beds and dramatic rock arrangements. Nothing remains of the palace and temple complexes, but remarkably there are sufficient vestiges of this garden to conjure up images of how it might have been used. These glimpses into the past are intriguing. Guests at great "winding-water" banquets would sit by streams that wove through meadows before entering the lake. Resplendent garden parties were held in which painted dragon barges, filled with musicians dressed in elaborate costumes, were rowed and punted around the lake. At special ceremonies, people might pray for rain to fall in

Above: *The garden of the Moss Temple at Saiho-ji was a 12th-century pond garden, with islands linked by wooden bridges. It has now become famous for its velvet carpets of moss.*

Left: *An ambitious waterfall scheme in the Rheinaue Garden, Germany, creates drama through well-observed rock arrangements and in the ways that the water spills over the rocks.*

Above left: *Recycled materials, such as these millstones, make beautiful stepping stones. Old temple pillar bases and sections are also popular in Japan.*

Above: *The gardens of the Heian shrine, in Kyoto, were created in the late 19th century to recreate the spirit of the 10th- and 11th-century gardens of the Heian period.*

order to water the rice fields, or they might evoke Amida Buddha in his Paradise garden.

The lakes of early pond gardens such as Motsu-ji were broad and well-lit, glimmering under the sun, moon and stars, while weeping willows swayed and shaded their banks. Birds and fish would have added movement and colour to this intoxicating scene. The lakes had a pebbled bottom or were edged with beaches of silver sand and backed by low hills planted with trees and shrubs. This style of pond garden differs from the later stroll gardens in having none of the more familiar tea houses, lanterns or water basins. Instead, the pond contained islands, often linked by bridges.

LATER POND GARDENS

Pond gardens remained popular in Japan, but as they became smaller, their outline became increasingly complex and indented and the rock arrangements more artistic and painterly. The sumptuous gowns of the ladies of the Heian period would have made it impossible for them to stroll around large lakeside gardens, and so in the Kamakura and Muromachi periods, ponds became smaller, and formed part of the first

KEY CONSIDERATIONS

Location	Choose the lowest part of the garden to make your pond, as this will look most natural and you will have a good view of the water.
Lining the pond	If you have room for a large pond, you can line it with clay and make it deep enough for boating. If your pond is small, line it with a butyl liner.
Surroundings	You will be able to use the soil dug out for the pond to make natural-looking small hills and undulating ground around the edges.
Edges	Use the natural contours of your pond to make beaches of cobbles or sand, caves or grottoes. A small sandy beach may be just the place to moor a small boat and launch it into the water.
Water flow	Ponds are usually filled by a natural or manmade stream. The water can be re-circulated using an electric pump. Different types of feeder stream will work well, from a flat meandering type to a steep waterfall.
Rocks	The placing of rocks in a feeder stream or waterfall and around the edges of a pond must be handled carefully. Try out the position of each rock until it looks perfectly natural in its setting, following the "request" or "desire" of the stone and bearing in mind which way the water will flow. Rocks can also be used as part of an island, particularly if you are making a crane or turtle shape, or as a bridge between the island and the mainland.
Extra features	Irises are the most common plants in Japanese ponds. You can also construct an island in your pond in an asymmetrical position, perhaps with a bridge linking it to the mainland.

Left: *Ponds, such as this one at Tenju-an, were used for boating parties, and were the central feature of all gardens until the appearance of dry gardens.*

TURTLE AND CRANE ISLANDS

Another common feature of the pond garden was the group of islands that represented the Isles of the Immortals. Some of these took the form of turtles and cranes. They can be included in today's gardens, although it is important to point out that Japanese representations of the crane or turtle are rarely naturalistic. The crane island is made up of a group of rocks, with one taller rock usually sitting up like a wing. In the groups of rocks representing turtles, the head and flippers are sometimes discernible, but more often the image is utterly abstract and only a trained eye can appreciate what is being depicted.

Turtle and crane motifs are not essential to a pond garden, but they can be included if they are treated with some sensitivity. To recreate a crane or turtle island, look at some famous examples. You will find that some are made entirely of groups of

Below: *Winding streams emulate a natural type of stream, with the rocks positioned to modulate the flow.*

real stroll gardens, a style of Japanese garden that we will look at later on. Most of these later pond and stream gardens were confined within walls, which meant that their size was fairly limited – a factor that makes it easier for us to envisage the practicalities of trying to create one in a smaller Western garden.

In trying to reproduce such a style, one has to imagine a far more poetic time, as well as one in which there was a far greater reverence for nature. While later gardens were influenced by painters and Zen philosophy, the Heian pond garden takes nature in its well-observed form as a principle feature in the design.

FOLLOWING NATURAL FORMS

The *Sakuteiki*, which was written in Heian times, names many forms of pond styles, islands, streams and waterfalls, and even notes the best techniques for planting trees. Even now, we can draw on this ancient work for inspiration when designing contemporary pond gardens. For example, when placing rocks or choosing the course of a stream, you need to follow the "desire" or "request" of the stone or water. Inanimate rocks were, and still are in Japan, thought to possess

personalities that must be treated with respect. By doing this, you will achieve a balanced and harmonious design for your garden.

It is also important to remember that the design of a water garden should be asymmetrical, even though the adjoining architecture may be symmetrical. This interplay between the formality of the architecture and the informality of the garden is part of the genius of Japanese gardens. The design of the pond is key, and achieving a pleasing shape is vital to the success of the finished pond.

rocks, while others are islands of earth with rocks protruding into the lake, which can be seen as flippers, a tail or a head. You are not aiming to create literal reproductions of these animals.

PINE ISLANDS

A favourite for Japanese gardens is a pine island, which is evocative of the windswept pine-clad islands of Matsushima, a scenic site in northern Japan, famous throughout Japanese garden history. Large pond gardens may include several pine islands of varying sizes, but if there is just one island, this could be reached by a traditional Chinese red-painted bridge, the most popular style of bridge when the Matsushima garden was made.

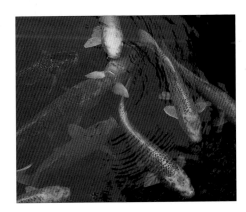

Above: *Japanese koi carp , considered to be a symbol of prosperity and good luck, were developed from the basic black carp, or* Magoi.

PLANNING A POND GARDEN

The pond or lake is the central feature of this style of garden and should be large enough and deep enough for a small boat, which can be kept moored to a stone or on view in an open-sided, ornate Chinese-style boathouse. There should be at least one island in the pond, often two, linked by bridges. By the 14th century, when ponds became smaller, the curved Chinese bridges were replaced by bridges made from less ornate materials such as rocks or unpainted timber. Small islands can be planted with pine trees or grasses.

The outline of the pond can be indented with coves, beaches and grottoes. The land around the pond might be hilly, with the hills planted naturalistically with groups of trees. You can easily create a pond garden planted with iris beds and dotted with well-placed rock arrangements, possibly with a gently sloping sandy beach area. Imagine recreating those splendid outdoor celebrations with an *al fresco* pond-side supper for friends, perhaps lit with some paper lanterns.

READING AROUND THE SUBJECT

There is a range of useful background reading material to help the gardener to understand the roots of the pond garden style. Despite their age, the

Above: *Placing a lantern at the end of a gravel spit is still a popular recreation of the famous natural scenic site of the Amanoshidate Peninsula on the north coast of Honshu.*

following books still have a place in the hearts of the Japanese.

• The *Sakuteiki* contains a wealth of practical ideas to inspire gardeners, with descriptions of streams, waterfalls and the symbolism of rock forms.

• *The Tales of Genji* by Murasaki Shikibu, written around the same time as the *Sakuteiki*, provides another important source of garden styles.

• *The Pillow Book* by Shonagon, also a contemporary of the *Sakuteiki*, makes amusing observations on the culture and gardens of the period.

Above: *A pine island in the tranquil lake setting of the Heian shrine, in Kyoto.*

Garden plan: a pond garden

The design of this pond garden would suit people with a large garden. The main feature is the pond fed by a winding stream or by a spring spilling over a waterfall. Pine islands and rocky islets are artfully placed, some of them reached by Chinese-style bridges and viewed from a pavilion that might double as a boathouse. The overall feel of the planting and rock placement is naturalistic.

MAKING A TURTLE ISLAND

Turtle and crane islands were built to lure the immortals to earth and learn their secrets, especially the recipe for the elixir of eternal youth. These islands can be made anywhere in a pond, just from a few well-placed rocks.

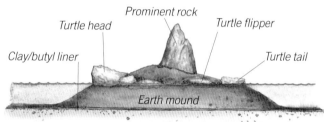

Turtle head / Prominent rock / Turtle flipper / Clay/butyl liner / Turtle tail / Earth mound

1 Make a rough sketch, then select rocks to represent the turtle parts. The island is the body of the turtle, made up of earth and a collection of supporting rocks. You also need rocks to represent the turtle's head and the four flippers. Just suggest the shape of the head and use wider rocks that reach out into the water at the four corners of the island for the flippers.

2 Construct the island before the pond is filled with water. You can build the island on a butyl liner, or add the liner after the island is complete, but if you are planning an elaborate arrangement then lay the liner first. If using machinery to transport the rocks and soil, you can roll back the butyl liner to avoid puncturing it. You can also lay out some extra layers of liner and underlay for protection.

3 Build the soil up in layers, making the base twice as wide as the island itself, so that the sides slope gently into the water. This will ensure that the rocks are sitting on stable ground. Place a ring of rocks just below water level around the soil to add stability.

4 Now place the rocks to signify the different parts of the turtle. Upright rocks will need to be buried by up to a third of their height to be stable and safe.

5 The island can then be planted with grasses and a pine tree. According to the myth, the turtle carries on its back one of the Isles of the Immortals. This could be represented by placing one particularly prominent rock on the "back" of the turtle.

Small hill with waterfall

Gravel path

Rocky

Small bridge over winding stream

Left: *Winding streams emulate a natural type of stream, with the rocks used to modulate the flow.*

Plant list

1 Black pine (*Pinus thunbergii*)

2 Cherry (*Prunus serrulata* varieties)

3 Japanese maple (*Acer palmatum*)

Rock groupings

Red Chinese bridge

Pine island with rocky shoreline

Rocky shoreline

Turtle island with Mount Horai

Rowing boat

Wooden boathouse

Left: *The arrangement of rocky islets is often taken from the myths of the Mystic Isles. This one is symbolic of Mount Horai.*

Left: *Heian garden buildings and bridges were often copies of those found in China at the time.*

Dry gardens

Dry gardens are often referred to as *kare-sansui*, which literally means "dry mountain water". This is a style of garden in which water has been replaced by sand, gravel or pebbles. These gardens have also become synonymous with what we now often call a Zen garden. Dry gardens were conceived by the Japanese with abstract designs, often just consisting of gravel, and as deeply spiritual and symbolic landscapes. They can also be enjoyed by visitors as peaceful and restorative environments where they can be appreciated for their calm beauty.

Above: *An unusual treatment for a dry garden at Shisendo, Kyoto. The fine sand has been brushed with a besom around a tree stump.*

THE HISTORY OF DRY GARDENS

Dry gardens have inspired garden designers throughout the world. An understanding or, better still, an experience of Zen will help you to find their spiritual essence, but another way to look at dry gardens is to see them as minimalist landscape art.

Before looking at the main features of the dry garden and how it can be successfully created in the West, it will be helpful to consider some of the historical, artistic and religious principles behind this unique garden style. The precise origins of such dry gardens remain a little obscure. References to dry landscapes occur as early as the 11th century, but they refer to the natural placement of rocks in grass or moss, and not to dry representations of water.

It is possible that the early Shinto shrines were a starting point. The great shrines at Ise stand in vast rectangles of gravel. This gravel was replaced every 20 years as part of the rituals of renewal and cleansing, while rocks were (and still are) used to represent the Buddha and the Buddhist Trinity. The earliest dry rock arrangements that preceded the *kare-sansui* may have been at Joeji-in, near Yamaguchi, where a collection of rocks was laid in an area of moss between the temple and the pond. This garden, which was created in the mid-1400s, is attributed to Sesshu, the great Japanese painter who reproduced his angular brush strokes in the garden using flat-topped and angular rocks. Sesshu was a monk, and also a painter and gardener, therefore possessing a rare

Below: *The rocks in this area of the garden at Nanzen-ji in Kyoto are arranged to display the innate quality of the stones.*

combination of talents. Looking at his paintings can be a source of inspiration even today.

These dry gardens were not created because of a natural absence of water. (Indeed, there is an abundance of water in many of the temple gardens around Kyoto. At the Ryoan-ji, for example, there is a large pond on the other side of the wall from the dry garden.) Instead, they were created for a mixture of artistic and philosophical reasons. The first reason was based on the example of Japanese painters, whose artistic work inspired gardeners to use a monochromatic treatment of the landscape, and the second was linked to the philosophy of Zen.

THE INFLUENCE OF ZEN

Most dry gardens appear in Zen temples and are therefore strongly associated with Zen Buddhism and meditation.

The dry gardens in Zen temples tend to be framed within rectangular courtyards close to the abbot's quarters (*hojo*). They can be viewed as paintings, illustrating distant and idealized landscapes "hung" within

Right: The garden of Tenju-an, in Kyoto, is a superb example of the interplay between geometric manmade and irregular natural forms.

Above: *The Mystic Isles rock arrangement at Tofuku-ji has immense power. The designer, Mirei Shigemori, used much larger and darker rocks than in more traditional arrangements.*

their rectangular frame. As garden style evolved throughout the 15th century, its influences shifted away from art as an inspiration for natural landscapes towards art as a means of teaching Zen tenets.

In Zen, one reaches one's true self by diverting one's gaze from the material to the spiritual world. Through

Above: *This garden near Kyoto was created in a small, rectangular framework. Raked sand and a single maple in a mossy mound prove how little you need to create a perfect scene.*

meditation, one can experience what is known as the "void", a formless state of no-self, which Zen defines as the original human state. Time spent in this state is a form of spiritual renewal. This "meditative void" can be equated to those areas of unpainted whiteness in a picture and to the empty space of raked sand in a dry

garden. Whereas lay people might look at a Zen garden and see islands in an ocean or mountain tops circled in mist, Zen practitioners will simply see space, a reflection of the infinite space that lies deep within us. Many of the arts of Zen employ the use of space to encourage this kind of self-awareness. The act of raking gravel is a meditative practice for Zen monks, while some Zen gardens include arrangements of rocks that signify aspects of Buddhism, for monks to contemplate.

RYOAN-JI

The Ryoan-ji garden, in Kyoto, is a timeless example of the exceptional degree of artistry and the deep understanding of the painters, monks and garden-makers of the late 15th century, when it is thought that this garden was constructed. The Ryoan-ji is a rectangular courtyard bordered on three sides by a clay and oil wall and on the fourth side by the abbot's quarters, where a long veranda overlooks the garden from about 75cm (30in) above the level of the garden. The area is about the size of a tennis court, and is neatly edged in a frame of blue-grey tiles. The whole of the inner space is spread with a fine, silvery grey quartzite grit that is raked daily along its length in parallel lines. This "sea" of sand is the background canvas to 15 rocks in five groups of 5-2-3-2-3 (see page 76), fringed by moss . This pattern recurs throughout the Far East, even in the rhythm of music and the chanting of Buddhist texts. The parallel lines of raked gravel break their pattern and form circles around the groups of rocks like waves lapping against island shores.

The magical way that the rocks are grouped and spaced has gripped generations of visitors, and not just monks, artists, poets and gardeners. No one knows the exact meaning of these groupings. Some have described them as a tiger taking her cubs across a river, while others see them as mountains in the mist or as islands

Above: *At Nanzen-ji, in Kyoto, over two-thirds of the dry garden is composed of sand. The rest is dedicated to this group of rocks and shrubs.*

Below: *The raked circles of sand in the Ryoan-ji garden represent the rough seas and the rocks the sacred mountains of the Mystic Isles.*

Right: *A simple dry garden using one bold and interestingly shaped rock and a small grove of carefully trimmed bamboo, in the grounds of Nijo castle, Kyoto.*

surrounded by sea. One reason for this puzzle is that Zen practitioners probably started with an idea, but ended up focusing on universal truths and abstract, natural shapes. When creating your own arrangements, bear in mind that the setting of the stones should follow their own "desire". The stones or rocks need not be particularly exceptional in themselves and should not be set as individual pieces of sculpture.

DESIGNING A DRY GARDEN

In the intial stages of planning a dry garden, first imagine a distant misty mountain landscape, a stream with waterfalls or a rocky shoreline. Look at how streams and rivers flow, how waves lap against rocks, and you will learn how to use the inspiration of nature to make raked gravel patterns around rocks.

Once you have composed a picture in your mind, then let go of the superfluous and simply allow the

Above: *Dry rock arrangements are often centred around a main stone, which may have symbolized the Buddha, the sacred mountain of Shimusen or Mount Horai of the Mystic Isles.*

essence of the composition to take over, and minimize it. Remember that an unfilled space is just as important as a space containing objects or plants. This "minimalism" has inspired many contemporary garden designers to reproduce the dry garden in modern urban environments. After all, dry gardens were often created in domestic courtyards, not just in Zen temples. A simple composition could be created with a rock or two, a stone lantern, a water basin and a section of bamboo fence set simply in a stretch of sand.

USING PLANTS IN THE DRY GARDEN

Dry gardens are not restricted to just sand, gravel and rocks – they also involve plants. At the garden of the Shoden-ji, in north-west Kyoto, rocks have been replaced by mounds of clipped azaleas in more or less the same kind of pattern as the rocks at the Ryoan-ji. The azaleas are clipped so much that they do not flower very well, but form is considered far more important than colour in this style of Japanese garden. If you liken these gardens to the monochrome paintings that inspired them, it is clear that colour is of little or no importance, while composition and space are paramount.

CONTEMPORARY INTERPRETATION

Dry gardens may appear to be quintessentially Japanese, but the appeal of their pared-down, minimalist style is both universal and contemporary. Once you have understood how and why the original 15th-century dry gardens were created, you may want to employ new, exciting methods of expressing the same principles, but in ways and with materials that are more relevant to your own culture and landscape.

Above: *The dry "silver" garden created by Gilles Clément at the Parc André Citröen in Paris is Japanese-inspired and represents a dry river bed planted with silver shrubs.*

Garden plan: a dry garden

The best place for a dry garden is a courtyard enclosed by walls or
fences. This contains the garden so it can be seen as a painting
"hung" within its frame, and protects it from the elements.
The deeper Zen meaning of these dry gardens is one of
emptiness of mind – a goal of Zen meditation. The whole
garden should possess an air of restraint and be a calm and
spiritual place of sand, rocks and maybe a few plants.

TOPIARY IN THE DRY GARDEN

The use of topiary to represent a landscape can be seen in some of
the great dry landscape gardens such as the Ryoan-ji or Shoden-ji.
A weathered pine might suggest a mountain or a seaside landscape,
and groups of clipped plants could symbolize a range of distant hills.

Shakkei *(borrowed scenery)*

Trees to
frame view

White-painted
plaster wall

Tile-topped
wall

Clipped azalea

Raked gravel

1 Make a sketch of the site and draw an outline of the landscape you
want to reproduce. This kind of design typically incorporates *shakkei*
(borrowed landscape), so look outside your garden to see if there is
anything you could integrate. Get further inspiration by looking
through a book on Chinese landscape painting. You may want to
reproduce a favourite landscape that is familiar to you.

2 Decide whether to buy small, young plants, which are cheaper
and easier to establish, but will take time to grow, or larger plants for
a more instant result. Use plants that will be different sizes, as a
variation in heights is effective. If you cannot obtain large azaleas,
you should be able to buy large plants of cheaper unclipped
boxwood, which you can clip to your own shape. Other evergreens
could be used, such as varieties of camellia, photinia or osmanthus.

3 If the soil on your site is poor or of the wrong type for azaleas,
which prefer acid soil, dig out generous holes for each plant.
Make sure that the area is well drained or put some gravel in the
bottom of the holes, then fill with the soil mix you require and
plant your specimen plants.

4 Spread the gravel and sand for the raked "dry water" effect.

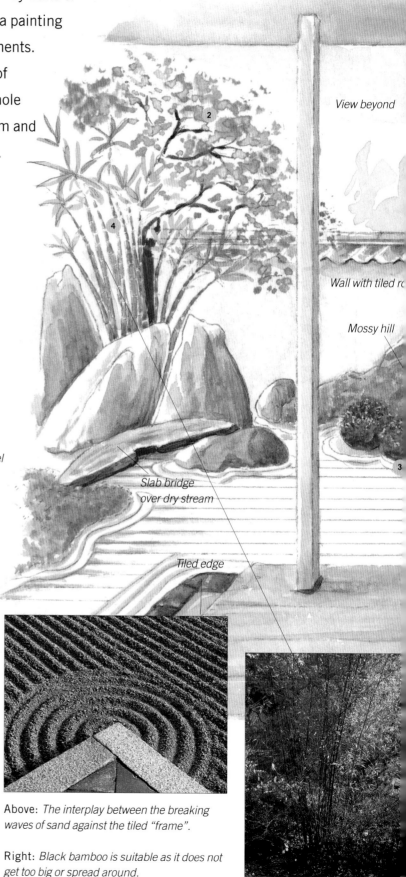

View beyond

Wall with tiled r[...]

Mossy hill

Slab bridge
over dry stream

Tiled edge

Above: *The interplay between the breaking
waves of sand against the tiled "frame".*

Right: *Black bamboo is suitable as it does not
get too big or spread around.*

Plant list

1 Japanese black pine (*Pinus thunbergii*)
2 Spring plum (*Prunus* species)
3 Clipped azalea
4 Black bamboo (*Phyllostachys nigra*)

Dry waterfall

Mossy hill

Plaster wall

Raked sand

Turtle island

Veranda

Right: *Mossy mounds may need frequent watering in order to keep them fresh and green.*

Right: *Clipped azaleas can have the same solid presence as standing rocks.*

Tea gardens

Tea gardens were designed as places in which to appreciate *sado*, the tea-drinking ceremony. These spaces were seen to represent a break in a journey from a busy urban centre to a secluded country retreat. The design and philosophy of the tea garden can easily be adapted for the modern garden, and suits city life now as much as it did in the 16th century. Each element of a tea garden – for example, the stepping stones, lanterns, water basins and even the tea house itself – can easily be created using modern materials.

Above: *Every tea garden has a* tsukubai *arrangement – a low water basin filled with fresh water and accompanied by a lantern.*

THE HISTORY OF TEA GARDENS

Tea, imported from China, had been drunk at the imperial court since the 9th century, but its cultivation did not start in Japan until the 13th century. The Buddhist monk Eisai, returning from pilgrimages to China, is credited with introducing both Zen Buddhism and tea plants to Japan.

Tea was drunk by Buddhist monks as an aid to wakefulness during their long hours of meditation. It also became popular among the poets, intellectuals, samurai and merchants at the end of the 15th century. The monks and intellectuals brought the worlds of Zen Buddhism, poetry, fine porcelain and art appreciation together into the theatre of tea drinking, and created what is known as the "tea ceremony", drawing the simple act of drinking tea into the realm of high art. By the mid-16th century, tea ceremonies, tea houses and tea gardens were part of the culture of Japan.

The first great tea masters of the 16th century built their tea houses to imitate the mountainside hermitages of the Chinese sages. These sages were learned in the arts, philosophies and religions of their time. The Japanese also built their own style of hermitage that evolved into the tea house, not in the mountains, but right in their back gardens in cities such as Kyoto, Nara and the port of Sakai, near present-day Osaka. The gardens

Below: *Tea houses are most often constructed from natural materials that are allowed to weather. This tea house has a tiled roof, whereas many others are thatched.*

Below: *A bamboo panel tied with jute is framed between two branches. At the step, guests remove their shoes before entering the tea house.*

around these "mountain places in the city", as they became known, were originally based on paths, symbolizing the routes taken by pilgrims on their way to meet sages in their hermitages. The tea garden, or *roji*, which means "dewy path" or "dewy ground", evokes those mountain paths and gradually evolved to include an elaborate set of sophisticated symbols.

The greatest tea master was the 16th-century Sen no Rikyu, who had a preference for the rustic and the rough. His successors, such as Furuta Oribe and Kobori Enshu, who created gardens in the early 17th century, were from the samurai class and had more of a taste for sophisticated manmade materials. By the 17th century, tea paths were often made of formal square paving and millstones. The tea houses also changed, becoming more refined, more open and less humble.

Later still, tea houses evolved into tea arbours, where tea might be drunk while looking out over the garden. The changing aesthetic from the Muromachi period through to the Edo period shows a slow evolution from *wabi-sabi* ("withered loneliness"), indicating a taste for the impoverished, to *asobi*, which is a more playful and artistic style.

THE TEA GARDEN RITUAL

After generally passing through a main gate, guests would enter the first half of the tea garden, known as the outer *roji*. They might then be asked to wait, often in a small shelter or booth, before being led deeper into the garden, then to the tea house. On the way, they might pass through a middle "stooping gate", perhaps with a lantern nearby, designed to force the guests to bow slightly – a moment of enforced humility to stimulate an awareness of the material world the

guests were leaving behind and of the higher, purer realms of consciousness they would encounter in the tea house.

After passing under the stooping gate, the guests would enter the inner *roji* that surrounded the tea house. This part of the garden was the "wilderness", which represented the wild mountain landscape that might surround a Chinese hermitage. The guests would

then wash their hands and mouths at a low basin called a *tsukubai* (or "stooping basin"). This a lower style of basin than the taller *chozubachi*, which is a water basin more frequently found near the veranda of the main house.

Below: *Planting in tea gardens is generally less tightly controlled and more suggestive of a wilderness.*

A lantern often accompanies the *tsukubai*, as many tea ceremonies took place in the evening.

After cleansing themselves, the guests would proceed to the tea house, remove their shoes and enter through a small hatch-like entrance, the *nigiriguchi*. This entrance was made too small for a samurai still wearing his sword to enter, so some tea houses had special racks built outside to hold swords. Once inside, the guests would admire a seasonal flower arrangement and a scroll hanging in an alcove, known as the *tokonoma*. The most important guest would sit with their back to the *tokonama*. The tea ceremony would then begin.

Above: *The style of the* roji, *or tea path, evolved over the centuries, from one that was natural and simple to a more artful and complex style, like this one at Nanzen-ji.*

CONSTRUCTION OF THE TEA HOUSE

The tea house was often built to look like a rustic thatched hut, but it was always constructed with the finest planed timber. Elegant rush matting, called *tatami*, lined the floor. The rustic appearance of the tea house, combined with the refinement of domestic and temple architecture, created a whole new language in garden architecture – a discipline that is still studied today.

THE FEATURES OF A TEA GARDEN

A tea garden can include a range of decorative features, such as gates, water basins and lanterns, as well as following certain aesthetic rules,

Left: *Inside the tea house or tea room is a specially designed alcove (*tokonoma*), decorated with a simple "country-style" flower arrangement and a calligraphy scroll.*

Right: *A waiting booth at Chikurin-in, a tea garden near Kyoto. This type of shelter is sited near the beginning of a tea path, as a place for guests to gather until invited to the tea house.*

such as an attention to detail and cleanliness, which are apparent in all Japanese gardens.

The tea house itself could be quite traditional in appearance, built with a thatched roof and sliding panels. One shogun even had a portable tea house built that was gilded throughout, as a symbol of his power. Thus, the basic principles of the tea garden could be adapted to suit the aspirations and taste of the owner.

TEA GARDENS IN MINIATURE

In small town gardens where space may not allow for a tea house, the Japanese will convert one room in the house into a tea room with a *tatami-*matted floor. For the tea garden they would still devise a path, or *roji*, that wanders through a "wilderness" of just a few paces from one door, then returning via a side door, perhaps with a *nigiriguchi*, into the tea room. The whole point is to be able to create an illusion of wandering through a wild mountainside. The onus is placed on the guests to comprehend that the journey they are taking is "real", but to help them, the garden designer will include pointers and hints as to the symbolic nature of each element.

If a whole *roji* is reduced to a few metres (yards) in length, it would still include a few stepping stones, a water basin, a lantern and one or two plants, such as a camellia or a bamboo, to suggest the wilderness. A rock might indicate a mountain, while a post might be enough to suggest a middle crawl-through gate (see page 172). That is the essence of the tea garden: creating a spiritual, rather than a literal, journey.

THE FLEXIBILITY OF THE TEA GARDEN

Once the significance of the tea garden has been grasped, you can be as creative as you want, just like the designers of the 16th century. While one tea master might have enjoyed a natural look, another might have preferred a creative mix of the manmade and the natural. Such adaptability is the main reason why tea houses and tea gardens never really died out, reappearing in stroll gardens and courtyard gardens to the present.

A tea garden does not have to be imbued with the tenets of Zen to be intriguing or even beautiful. Indeed, when Zen Buddhism went out of favour in Japan and Confucianism was in the ascendancy, the tea ceremony continued to thrive, but it evolved to express a more outward and cultured refinement than the deeper inner transformative power of Zen. This illustrates just how flexible the concept of the tea ceremony and garden can be, and that it can easily be reinterpreted to accommodate virtually any culture.

When you are creating a tea garden of your own, you could make a simple layout with just a few scattered rocks, bamboos, natural paving and bamboo

gates, or a much more elaborate affair. You could build your own tea house, to whatever level of complexity and authenticity you want, or you could simply convert any garden building into a tea house, even with chairs and tables, although the space should be kept clean and treated with a certain degree of reverence, so that you can entertain guests in a quiet and respectful atmosphere. All you really need for a tea garden is a path.

Right: *A waiting booth (*koshikake*) in the inner tea garden, or* roji, *at Chishaku-in, Kyoto. This simple square construction has a thatched reed and bamboo roof and a pair of benches.*

Garden plan: a tea garden

The principles of making a tea garden can be adapted to almost any space. The main feature is the path of stepping stones inside the main gate that leads to the tea house via a waiting room, past lanterns and water basins, and through intervening gates. The garden should become wilder as the path approaches the tea house. This, as in so many of the Japanese arts, is achieved symbolically rather than literally.

THE MIDDLE CRAWL-THROUGH GATE

This gate is placed halfway through the tea garden between the inner and outer *roji*. In leaving the everyday world for the spiritual world, the guest is forced to bow their head, either under a low lintel or, as in the style of gate described below, by pushing their way under it.

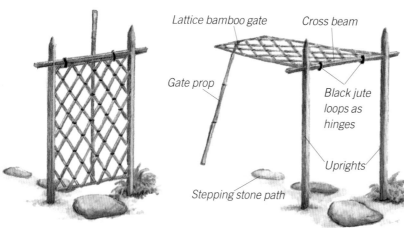

Lattice bamboo gate
Cross beam
Gate prop
Black jute loops as hinges
Uprights
Stepping stone path

Waiting room

Outer *roji*

Stepping stone path

Entrance gate

1 Using the gate as a guide, mark where the two upright posts will be. They should be 7.5–10cm (3–4in) square or round and 2.5m (8ft) long.

2 Dig holes 60–70cm (24–28in) deep for the posts. If the soil is firm, simply firm the two posts in around the bases. In loose ground, you should concrete the base of the two posts.

3 Measure the height of the gate, and trim off the tops of the two posts to the right height.

4 Fix the cross beam (which should be the same width as the posts and 1m [1yd] long) on top of the posts, creating mortise-and-tenon joints, by drilling holes for a piece of dowelling and pushing it through, or by screwing the crossbeam down with two 15cm (6in) screws on to each post.

5 Hang a lightweight bamboo gate, 1.5–2m (5–6½ft) high, on to the cross beam using some thick black jute for hinges.

6 Attach a bamboo pole 4cm (1½in) in diameter and 2.5m (8ft) long to the base of the gate. This pole will be used to prop the gate open.

Left: *Guests rest in a waiting room before the host invites them to go into the tea house itself.*

Lavatory

Tied rock

Bamboo
fence

9

Well

Inner roji

2

Rock
Moss

Moss

Tsukubai

Lantern

8

6

3

Plant list

1 *Enkianthus perulatus*
2 Clipped azalea
3 Autumn-flowering
   camellia (*Camellia
   sasanqua*)
4 Sedge (*Carex*)
5 Domestic bamboo
   (*Nandina domestica*)
6 Red pine (*Pinus
   densiflora*)
7 Japanese black pine
   (*Pinus thunbergii*)
8 Japanese maple (*Acer
   palmatum*)

Left: *A fence and
gate along the tea
path divide the
garden into two
halves. This one is
a hinged bamboo
gate, but could
equally be a middle
crawl-through gate.*

Left: *The* tsukubai,
*or "crouching
basin", is always
accompanied by
a lantern.*

Stroll gardens

A stroll garden is one in which the visitor is encouraged to amble slowly along paths that circle around a small pond or lake. Although there had been stroll gardens in Japan since the 14th century, they came to the fore in the Edo period of the 17th century and beyond. Unlike the earlier pond and stream gardens, where the emphasis was on the water, and boating was the main activity, the emphasis in a stroll garden was on the paths that wound among a new set of garden motifs. Classic examples are all large gardens, but, as long as there is room to wander, smaller ones are possible.

Above: *Most stroll gardens have a path that circles around a central pond, with specially contrived views at strategic points.*

THE HISTORY OF STROLL GARDENS

The stroll garden is one of the most familiar Japanese garden styles, partly because it incorporates so many aspects of other styles. You will find stepping-stone paths, lanterns, water basins and tea houses from the tea garden; expanses of sand with a rock or two, usually near the main building, from the dry garden; and the use of water in streams, waterfalls and ponds from the pond garden. Other elements might include bamboo fences and bridges of all kinds. The tea houses, tea arbours, lanterns, bridges and contrived views of scenes reproduced from historic or famous places around Japan or even China that could be found here were all carefully placed to entertain the stroller.

When the stroll garden was developed in the 17th century, the pervasive aesthetic of the times was not as "spiritual" as that of the earlier dry and tea gardens. There was more of a sense of playfulness (*asobi*) as well as a desire for the sumptuous and magnificent, and Japanese garden owners prided themselves on their connoisseurship of the arts.

Nevertheless, stroll gardens managed not to be overly ostentatious because they still employed the restraint and cultivated poverty of many of the aspects of the tea garden. This restraint in garden design was known as *shibumi* (meaning "astringent"), which underlined their markedly minimalist, unpretentious and subdued beauty. *Shibumi* is a term that can also be used to describe many contemporary Japanese gardens.

Although some of the gardens of the *daimyos* (land-owning lords) were somewhat grandiose, there were other, smaller gardens that were delightfully playful in their use of plants, water and architecture. A stroll garden could be as large as 20 hectares (50 acres) or be created in as little as 25sq m (about a sixteenth of an acre). Through the careful use of space and meandering paths, smaller areas can be made to look much larger than they actually are. One device that was commonly practised in stroll gardens was the "borrowing" of scenery, such as distant buildings and hills outside the bounds of the garden, as part of the garden plan – a technique known as *shakkei* (see page 30).

In the years following the fall of the Tokugawa shogunate at the end

Left: *Azaleas in flower in the small stroll garden at Shisendo, Kyoto. A simple garden, it has fine sand paths, rounded azaleas and a small pool with irises.*

of the Edo period and the emperor's restoration as the head of state (Meiji period), there was a return to more romantic ideals, as seen in the Heian period 1,000 years earlier. Some of these late-19th-century stroll gardens adopted a more naturalistic form, in which streams were designed to look like those found in wooded mountains. This style was more appealing to Western gardeners than the earlier very prim and trimmed stroll gardens.

ROCKS AND TOPIARY

In most stroll gardens, rocks played a far less prominent role than they had in the earlier Kamakura and Muromachi periods, partly because the Edo period was based on the new capital, Edo (Tokyo), where rocks were far scarcer than they had been around the previous capital, Kyoto. This scarcity led garden designers to rely more on clipped shrubs for dramatic form. This distinctive form of topiary, known as *o-karikomi*, is a fine

Above: *The 19th-century garden of Murin-an is full of illusions. A pair of wild-looking mountain streams appear almost like great rivers flowing through the "hills" of azalea.*

art that is still practised extensively today. All kinds of plants were clipped: shrubs were trimmed into hedges or rounded forms like small hills, and sometimes huge evergreens were carved into abstract shapes. These mounds of clipped shrubs were mostly azaleas and

Left: *A mass of clipped azaleas is typical of the planting style in Edo-period stroll gardens. A few rocks are interspersed among them, but rocks feature less prominently than in earlier styles. This was because rocks were scarce around the then new capital of Edo, present-day Tokyo.*

Right: *An early Edo-period stroll garden in Kyoto. Here the rocks are dramatic and symbolic of the power of the shogun, Tokugawa Ieyasu, who built this garden at Nijo Castle, with the exaggerated masses as a statement of his own prestige.*

Left: *The 14th-century garden of the Tenryu-ji was one of the first pond-style gardens with strolling paths, but this was a period when the natural placement of rocks was the key feature.*

Below: *Larger stroll gardens often include groves of cherries, plums or peaches, whose blossoms are especially celebrated in spring.*

camellias, but any number of different evergreens might be employed and, occasionally, even deciduous shrubs such as enkianthus, whose leaves glow fiery red in the autumn.

When rocks were used in a stroll garden, they might be smaller stones strung like beads along the edge of ponds or used as stepping stones along paths or across inlets. Some of these stones were recycled architectural fragments such as temple pillar bases, old bridge supports or millstones. This practice of recycling materials was known as *mitate* ("to see anew").

VIEWING POINTS

Although stroll gardens are designed to be walked around, they are also meant to be viewed from the main house or from arbours in the garden. Traditional Japanese houses had verandas, raised above ground level, from which you look over an expanse of brushed or raked sand stretching as far as the pond. At the near edge of the pond you will find clipped azaleas and an occasional rock. Distant shores might be overhung by pines, their branches supported by posts.

STREAMS

At one end of the pond, a stream might enter, with a wide estuary traversed with stepping stones. These may be made from natural stone or formal slabs. Bridges that cross over streams or inlets can be a single slab of curved, carved granite, or a curved wooden bridge, sometimes painted red like a Chinese bridge. In more naturalistic settings, log bridges or natural stone can be used. The stream babbles over pebbles as it enters the pond. Further upstream, it is narrower, tumbling between rocks and over waterfalls, and hugged by ferns and sedges.

If you are blessed with a natural fall of land, you can create a stream that follows the slope of the ground.

Left: *A lantern sits on a promontory, playing the role of a lighthouse. Lanterns, in varied styles, are often strategically placed around the strolling paths, near gateways and at the base of hills.*

KEY CONSIDERATIONS

Ponds   These are usually the main feature of the stroll garden, to which all paths eventually lead via a wandering route. Ponds can include small islands with bridges and may be fed by a stream or waterfall.

Paths   The design of the main path is essentially to circle the pond, visiting or passing through various features, views and buildings on its way. Smaller paths may take off from this main path, leading to tea houses or to other main garden features.

Plants   The designer can celebrate the seasons through many wonderful Japanese plants, such as cherries, azaleas, wisterias, maples, irises, hydrangeas, pines of all kinds and a host of herbaceous plants such as miscanthus and Japanese anemones. Cherries, plums and maples might be planted in groves for the greatest impact; irises grow well in the estuaries to the pond or in a stream; hydrangeas flourish in the wooded shade of cryptomerias or maples; while grasses, anemones and toad lilies might poke out from among rocks or by the water's edge.

If your garden is flat, you can still create the illusion of a mountain or hillside from which a stream might naturally flow. In most cases, you will need a pump to recycle and oxygenate the water, especially if your pond is stocked with fish such as koi and carp, but the water should be kept fairly shallow, only about 60cm (2ft) deep, so the fish can be easily seen. Deeper bays and shelters can be built to give the fish some shade and protection in the extreme heat or cold.

THE ROUTE TO THE TEA HOUSE

If you plan to make a tea house or arbour, your visitors will be drawn along paths of stepping stones, guided by bamboo fences and through gates, past lanterns and water basins, to the tea house itself. Tea arbours are more open than tea houses, as they were used for less formal occasions where the emphasis was on a commanding view of the garden. Other buildings might include a thatched umbrella shelter or a Chinese-style hexagonal summerhouse. Paths may pass through groves of cherries or maples, sometimes in an open grassy glade, or under-carpeted with moss where the shade is deeper.

DESIGNING A STROLL GARDEN

Although stroll gardens can include many elements, the individual components should not distract from the whole. The plan can simply include a path, a pond, a few clipped shrubs, a lantern and some trees, such as maples, pines or cherries. Decorative elements such as flowering plants or statues should be used with care and restraint.

Even though stroll gardens may lack the spirituality of other styles, they obey certain rules of balance, and look to nature or famous scenes for their inspiration. When planning a garden in this style, focus on a simple design that includes a well-shaped pond and an interesting path, rather than an assorted handful of Japanese artefacts.

Above: *Although generally they are more elaborate and impressive, stroll gardens often include features found in earlier pond gardens, such as the stone bridge here.*

Right: *The azaleas in the stroll garden of Murin-an are clipped into abstract shapes and dispersed quite randomly.*

Garden plan: a stroll garden

A stroll garden can be made in a relatively small space. If you start with a flat site, small hills can be built up using the soil dug out when the pond is made. The path can wander around these hills and by the edge of the pond. The weaving path will lure the strolling visitor to arbours and vantage points to view cherry groves, waterfalls or iris beds, or to entice them over a natural stone bridge.

Hexagonal thatched arbour

7

6

Clipped hedge

Stepping-stone path

HOW TO BUILD NATURAL STONE STEPS

Steps can be created from naturally found rocks or large stones. When building the steps, always start from the bottom and work uphill. Design your steps to follow the natural shape of the garden, allowing them to change direction from time to time. Over long stretches, add the occasional platform or bench as a resting place.

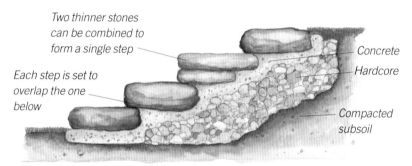

Two thinner stones can be combined to form a single step

Concrete

Hardcore

Each step is set to overlap the one below

Compacted subsoil

1 Measure the vertical and horizontal distances that you need the steps to climb. If you take the average of each stone you have available you can work out the number you will need. The steps should be flat, and the ideal dimensions are 10–15cm (4–6in) risers and 40–100cm (16–40in) treads. With Japanese-style steps these dimensions can vary with each step to make them appear more natural.

2 Dig out to a depth of 10cm (4in) below the lowest step, and lay a 10cm (4in) thick layer of concrete (one part cement to six parts concreting aggregate). Lay the first stone on this concrete slab.

3 If the ground is solid and the hill is not constructed artificially, you may not need the concrete mix, but you will need to firm the soil well as you go. On made-up ground, dig out all the loose soil to a depth of at least 30cm (12in) and backfill on to the compacted subsoil with hardcore, leaving enough room to add the 6–7.5 cm (2½–3in) depth of concrete for each step. Make sure the hardcore is rammed solid.

4 The front edge of each of the stones that you add should rest on the back of the previous one. This will ensure greater stability and will also appear more natural.

5 Set one step at a time, but be careful not to stand on them as you build the next one. For a long stretch it is advisable to build five or six steps at a time, then leave the concrete to set over two days before continuing. If you are building without concrete this will not be necessary.

Above: *Lanterns may be placed on promontories as the watchful symbol of the lighthouse.*

Above: *Recycled materials (mitate) such as these millstones make beautiful stepping stones.*

Plant list

1 *Iris ensata*

2 *Wisteria floribunda*

3 Clipped azaleas

4 Weeping cherry trees
(*Prunus subhirtella
pendula*)

5 Japanese maple (*Acer
palmatum*)

6 Bamboo

7 Red pine (*Pinus
densiflora*)

8 Japanese black pine
(*Pinus thunbergii*)

Cherry grove

Flowering wisteria arbour

Moss

Mixed hedge

Waterfall

Carp
stone

Pebble bottom

Rocks

Millstone stepping
stones

Water

Iris beds

yatsuhashi
bridge

Solid granite slab bridge

Dry sand garden

Pond outlet

Hooped bamboo strips

Right: *Waterfalls
and pond inlets in
stroll gardens are
built with naturalism
and artistry.*

Left: *There are many
styles of bridge in
wood or stone. A
single slab of stone
looks very natural.*

Courtyard gardens

The history of the courtyard garden starts in the early 17th century, but for contemporary designers the small, enclosed space adjoining a building still offers fantastic design possibilities. The design is generally simple, sometimes planned as a light extension to the house with large windows and doors, sometimes as a usable outdoor space. Small courtyard gardens, designed to be viewed through glass panels or set within atriums open to the sky, are now being created everywhere from large museums and corporate headquarters to private homes.

THE FIRST COURTYARD GARDENS

In the Heian period, courtyard gardens, or *tsubos*, were simple, small, enclosed spaces, perhaps inhabited by a single plant. The rooms that overlooked them, and the courtyards themselves, were named after these plants: the

Below: *Courtyard gardens borrow motifs from other styles, such as the rocks and sand of the dry garden and the stepping-stone path of the tea garden.*

Imperial Palace of Sento, in Kyoto, still has a Wisteria Court. Although the medieval residences of the samurai would have had *tsubos*, it was the rise of the merchant class in the late 16th century and throughout the Edo period that led to the refinement of the art of the courtyard garden (*tsubo-niwa*) in the early 17th century.

The small Edo courtyard gardens, like the much larger stroll gardens of the same period, were amalgams of

Above: *Courtyard gardens in contemporary settings can give a designer the chance to experiment with new materials.*

preceding garden styles, but they often lacked the coherent principles and philosophies that lay behind their parent styles. For instance, when the inspiration was a tea garden, tea paths were rarely used, nor did religion play a role. Instead courtyard gardens appropriated the motifs and artefacts

of previous styles. Where it was not possible to build a tea house, a room in the house might be used. The journey to this room could be via a "path" (*roji*) that would lead guests on a detour through the "wilderness" in the garden to maintain the illusion that they were heading somewhere special.

As the Edo period progressed, the insularity of the shogun's policies made the landed nobility (*daimyo*) poorer, while the merchants accumulated great wealth. The merchants were afraid to show off their money, as they could have had it confiscated, despite their importance within the national economy. In those days, the merchants were considered to be the lowest class; this was to prevent them from using their money to exert too much influence. Consequently, they constructed modest shop fronts to conceal a complex world of deep rooms and small enclosures, passages and courtyard gardens (*machiya*) hidden from the public in a style that made incredibly economic use of space. Some of these original gardens can still be seen in cities throughout Japan, but more such small gardens are being built today, often owing to lack of space

Above: *An entrance garden to the Silver Pavilion (Ginkaku-ji) in Kyoto illustrates the exceptional artistry of combining natural forms with the geometric.*

Below: *This Zen-style hotel courtyard has two shapes set in the sand: a grass circle and a grass gourd shape. These shapes are recognized symbols of hospitality.*

Below: *This tiny garden at Sanzen-in is a welcome island of green in the centre of the building, where there is only just enough light for plants such as ferns, mosses and bamboos to grow.*

Left: *This lush garden is located in Okinawa. The rear courtyard is enclosed by the L-shaped building, and by the successive layers of garden against a steep slope.*

explored Japan in the mid-19th century were astonished by the stroll gardens, but were equally amazed by these beautiful small town gardens.

Temple complexes also had *tsubo-niwa* gardens, usually simple dry gardens with one or two rocks and a "pool" of raked gravel. So, too, did restaurants, where narrow passageways were made into elaborate gardens with stone paving bordered by lanterns and clipped evergreens such as azaleas, mahonias, nandinas and bamboos. These gardens were, and still are, invariably too shady and too small for most flowering shrubs or cherries, limiting the range of plants to glossy evergreen shrubs such as aucubas, fatsias and camellias, as well as shade-loving ferns, bamboos and farfugiums. There is also often a carpeting of moss, just as would have been found in a traditional tea garden with its shady walks and scattered rocks.

rather than out of any need to hide them – making this style of garden particularly relevant today.

In addition to the entranceway garden, if there was one, most of the original merchants' houses featured a small central garden, which served to separate the trading area from the living quarters, and an even smaller courtyard garden termed a *tsubo-niwa*.

TSUBO-NIWA

The term *tsubo-niwa* derives from a measurement that is equivalent to 2 *tatami* mats. Many Japanese today still measure their houses and rooms in *tatamis*, approximately 1.85 x 0.9m (6 x 3ft), a measurement close to that of the average human being when lying down. So a *tsubo* is roughly 3.3sq m (18sq ft) – an indication of just how small these gardens can be.

THE ELEMENTS OF A COURTYARD GARDEN

In addition to their aesthetic appeal, minuscule courtyard gardens perform the important role of bringing light and air into the home, while the verandas running around their edges join together the *machiya*'s various areas. Though tiny in scale, the quality of the garden's lanterns, rocks and other components were and still are clear indicators of the taste and affluence of the *machiya*'s occupants.

Through the use of sliding screens, fence panels and bamboo blinds, it is possible to view these internal gardens from different angles, with each aspect framed within the rectilinear bounds of doors and window frames. The distinction between indoors and outdoors disappears. Westerners who

Above: *Dry gardens can give surprising life to inner courtyards where few plants would grow. The great waves of sand add a sense of movement in this garden at Ryogen-in.*

Another form that a courtyard garden might take is to create a scenic picture with miniature landscapes (*shakkei*) created to be viewed from one of the surrounding rooms.

A MODERN INTERPRETATION

In many ways, the courtyard style – a hybrid between the dry garden and the tea garden – suits the modern world well, and is often highly refined. Some of these gardens have everything from lanterns, water basins, small bridges, gravel and rocks to shady plants and sections of fencing used as a partition or to create privacy. Intricate journeys are hinted at, but it's never more than a hint. Courtyard gardens are often interpreted in a minimalist style today, maybe consisting simply of a single clump of bamboo planted off-centre or a group of rocks with ferns and moss. In fact the courtyard garden is an ideal medium for the contemporary garden designer, as the minimalist style is now so popular.

Roof gardens can also be classified as courtyard gardens, even though they may include views over the outside world. The raw, open, soil-less space on top of a building is perfect for the dry-landscape treatment, particularly where there are worries that excess weight from plants, pots, soil and water might damage the building's structure. The use of sand, lightweight plants and even fibreglass rocks in the Japanese style is often the ideal solution to this.

THE VERSATILITY OF THE COURTYARD GARDEN STYLE

In a sense, the courtyard garden can provide anything you want it to. It can be a dry garden, a tiny tea garden, a miniature landscape, or simply an area that encapsulates nature as a motif, or even a tranquil contemplative space. The courtyard garden can be both a retreat from the busy streets outside and an opportunity for escapist fantasy. It may also function in a mundane pragmatic way, simply by allowing more light to be drawn into the surrounding rooms.

In its design, the courtyard garden absorbs the best of Japanese culture, where one often sees one art form impacting on another. Just as a

flower arrangement may influence a tea room, so too does the tea ceremony influence the nature of the garden, and so on. Once we appreciate one art form, we will gain a better understanding of another. This cross-pollination is also at the heart of the courtyard garden style – an art form that is itself in a constant process of evolution.

Above: *The corner of this courtyard garden combines the rocks and gravel from a dry garden style with an oribe lantern, a popular feature of the tea garden.*

Above: *Most Japanese gardens use a grey-white quartzite grit, but this modern garden uses red gravel. Mirei Shigemori designed this garden in the Tofuku-ji temple complex in the 1950s.*

Garden plan: a courtyard garden

Courtyard gardens, or *tsubo-niwa*, can be made in the most unpromising sites, in narrow passages or in places where little light can reach. They often include elements from other garden styles, such as sand and rocks from the dry garden, or stepping-stone paths, lanterns and basins from the tea garden (with careful consideration of the miniature scale). Plants could include a clipped pine, an azalea, bamboo and a few ferns. The gardens are usually enclosed within walls or fences.

CREATING A *SHUKKEI*

The art of *shukkei*, which literally means "concentrated view", is most often found in courtyard gardens, especially in the form of a *kare-sansui* (dry-mountain-water) design made up of stones, gravel and clipped plants. The aim is to reduce an entire landscape scene to a miniature scale.

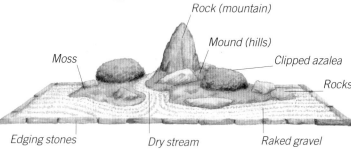

Rock (mountain)
Mound (hills)
Moss
Clipped azalea
Rocks
Edging stones
Dry stream
Raked gravel

Glass

Above: *Sleeve fences are used to deflect or to help frame a view.*

1 When choosing and planning your location note that *shukkei* should be laid out over a level site. The scenery can then be built up using small amounts of soil and rocks to suggest mountain and hill ranges. To do this, make small mounds of earth into which you will "plant" your rocks. Choose rocks that have credible mountain shapes. Some of these rocks can be almost buried, leaving exposed areas to look like escarpments.

2 Re-work the soil after placing the rocks to create a realistic undulation of hills and valleys, leaving indentations around the edges at ground level where you might expect seas and rivers to have eroded the natural forms.

3 Plant azaleas or boxwood, which can be clipped into mound or hill shapes, around the rocks and on the mounds. You can also add a wizened old pine to suggest an open weathered mountainside. Plant the earth with pieces of moss if you can find some, or with dwarf "dragon's beard" (*Ophiopogon*).

4 Spread gravel and sand around the level area to suggest an area of sea or a lake, drawing some of the sand into the scenery you have created where rivers might flow.

Veranda

Right: *Tall water basins (chozbachi) are often placed where they can be reached from the veranda. Long-handled ladles of metal or carved bamboo are usually laid across them, along with a bamboo lattice to prevent leaves from falling in.*

Lantern

Sleeve
fence

Stone

Large rock

Mossy mound

Water basin

Step down

Stepping stones

Sand

Bamboo fence

Plant list

1 Clipped bamboo
(*Phyllostachys nigra
henonis*)

2 Soft shield fern
(*Polystichum
setiferum*)

3 Clipped azalea

4 Hart's tongue fern
(*Asplenium
scolopendrium*)

5 Red pine (*Pinus
densiflora*)

Left: *Stepping stones
across sand look
effective when
surrounded by moss.
These paths may be
used for tea ceremonies,
where guests will leave
the house by one door,
and walk along the path
into a specially prepared
tea room.*

Left: *This high bamboo
fencing gives a clear
definition to the edge
of the courtyard.*

NATURAL MATERIALS

In the Japanese garden, the shapes of nature are celebrated, with great prominence typically given to one beautifully shaped rock or boulder set in subtly coloured gravel. This chapter looks at the natural materials that commonly feature in Japanese gardens. It explains how to source them, how to use them and also offers useful step-by-step features and practical illustrations to demonstrate specific techniques and designs. Paving and stepping stones are used, both decoratively and to create pathways. Gravel, grit and sand are also essential, traditionally designed to imitate the whiteness of a painter's canvas and the flow of water. In combination with rocks, gravel and sand form the vocabulary for the familiar dry-water features of the Japanese garden, such as waterfalls and streams, that are also illustrated here.

Ground cover, in particular moss, and the use of plants both make an important contribution. Moss grows profusely in Japan and is a natural ground cover that allows more freedom with planting than grass. While some gardens eschew the use of plants altogether, especially with dry garden designs, certain garden plants, such as azaleas, are used as substitutes for rocks or are clipped to imitate distant hills using the art of topiary.

Above: *Cobbles feature strongly in dry gardens.*
Left: *The intrigue of a Japanese garden is largely to do with natural forms, used in artful imitation of nature.*

Rocks & boulders

Rocks have formed the foundation of the Japanese garden from the earliest days. No other culture has made rocks so central to its garden art. It is possible to trace the history of the placement of rocks, from their first use in shrines and later as motifs for sacred mountains to their grouping in and around water. Later, in the dry gardens of the Muromachi period (1393–1568), water was replaced by sand, while in the gardens of the Edo period (1603–1867) rocks were replaced by clipped shrubs, which were used to imitate hills and mountains.

SPIRITUAL QUALITIES AND SYMBOLISM
Rocks were originally thought to possess spirits and the ability to draw the gods down to earth. They were later used to represent the mountain homes of the immortals, as well as the Buddha and his attendants. However, Zen monks, who had little time for superstition, rejected much of the esoteric symbolism of rocks and gave them more philosophical and decorative roles.

Above: *The central rock in this arrangement represents the Buddha, with two subservient attendant stones.*

Below: *The scale and quantity of these rocks at Nijo Castle were intended to express the power of Ieyasu Tokugawa (1543–1616) in the early 1600s.*

Although rocks were, and still are, placed in symbolic groups, they now tend to be arranged according to certain aesthetic rules. It takes a well-trained and experienced eye to read the symbolism in a group of stones. Groups of rocks that appear entirely natural may actually possess a number of possible symbolic meanings. Therein lies the genius of the Japanese rock-setters. Do not let this put you off creating symbolic arrangements in your own garden. Historians and Zen practitioners may like to read complex messages in classic rock arrangements, but it is not necessary to have such a deep understanding to compose successful groupings. It was, after all, the study of Chinese and Japanese minimalist ink-and-brush paintings that inspired them. Take a look at some of those paintings. The important thing to remember is that less is more, and not to be too decorative in your approach. What you leave out is almost more important than what you put in, and neither the stones nor the plants need be fancy or remarkable in themselves.

CREATING A ROCK GARDEN

We are fortunate that the Japanese have always rated rocks so highly because excavations of ancient gardens can still give a good idea of what they looked like, and this may help with the placement and grouping of the rocks. One garden in the city of Nara, 48km (30 miles) south of Kyoto, which was excavated in the 1970s (see picure on page 10), was found to be over 1,000 years old. There, the rocks are arranged in a surprisingly naturalistic way around a pond and stream, providing us with a useful example to follow.

Above right: *Gleaming rocks form a dramatic centrepiece in this* ryu-ten *("teashop in the garden") in Koraku-en, in Okayama.*

Right: *The setting of rocks, usually within gravel, the latter often representing the sea, is the central creative dynamic in the making of most Japanese gardens.*

Avoid using rocks with fantastic shapes. These have never been popular in Japan, except during a brief Edo/Confucian period. Chinese gardeners, in general, were much keener on using fantastic sculptural rocks, many of which were raised from lake beds, standing them on pedestals as symbols of immortality. The Japanese, on the other hand, are more interested in discovering a rock's natural inner essence.

From a design point of view, there is endless scope when working with larger rocks, but don't get carried away with design ideas and remember the inner essence of the rocks if you wish to achieve a natural effect that does not jar with the rest of the setting you have created in your garden.

MAKING ROCK GROUPINGS

Rocks are generally placed in groups. Seven was an auspicious number to the Chinese, as it is in many cultures, and was the original number of the Mystic Isles. Music was composed in units of 7-5-3 beats, while the prayers recited to Buddha Amida were chanted 7, 5 and 3 times in succession. By the 15th century, all kinds of objects were arranged in groups of 15, including rocks. The Ryoan-ji, for instance, is a 5-2-3-2-3 arrangement.

Most groups will consist of one main stone and up to five accessory stones, with one or more unifying stones to stabilize the group. Others might be used as linking stones to join together the members of one group, as well as different groups. The accessory stones can be placed to the front, rear or side of the main stone, huddled up against it or

Below: *The garden of the Ryoan-ji was first laid out in 1499. The composition of 15 rocks is set in a rectangle of sand, against a backdrop of an oil and clay wall overhung with trees.*

Above: *At the Konchi-in, in Kyoto, the eye is drawn to the rocks as they sit in the centre of a layered composition, with its foreground of raked sand and backdrop of evergreens.*

some distance away, but should never obscure it. Try making the attendant stones respond to or echo the angle or position of the main stone. These stones should respond to the energy of the main stone in one of the following seven ways:

Receptive A rock that is placed to receive the energy from the main stone that is leaning towards it.

Transmitting An attendant rock that transmits energy from the main stone towards others in the group.

Pulling A rock that is angled to counteract a main stone that leans away from it.

Pursuing Set behind a main stone that leans away from it, this rock is angled in the same direction, as if following it.

Stopping An upright main stone is stabilized by an accompanying one.

Attacking The accompanying rock leans towards a neutral, upright main stone.

Flowing This rock is a passive conductor rather than a more active transmitter; often flat, it acts as a kind of conduit to others.

These terms are not meant to be rigid, but they help to describe the relationship of the stones to each other and to clarify what might work in a particular grouping. They also highlight the subtle approach that is required to make such a grouping work. If your grouping does not look right, then work through these terms to help give the stones an authentic Japanese touch.

By far the best way of learning how to arrange rocks, however, is by studying good, authentic examples. Because of the static nature of rocks, it is possible to do this from looking at photographs, but note that arrangements must look good from any angle (which a photograph might not show), although they will tend to have one front side that gets the most attention. Also bear in mind that it is better not just to copy an arrangement but to be creative, seeking out and following the "desires" of your own particular rock.

USING ROCKS IN THE JAPANESE GARDEN

The placement and grouping of rocks is crucial to the authenticity of a Japanese garden. The following guidelines should help you:

• study Japanese gardens, in pictures or by visiting good examples;

• go and look at rocks in the wild, by the sides of streams with boulders, or at the seaside. Make sketches of their natural arrangements if you can;

• avoid strange-shaped rocks. It's better to find rocks that would look good grouped together rather than one dominating specimen;

• trust your own instincts and don't be intimidated by the fact that it is such an ancient art and that rocks are supposed to be spiritual and symbolic;

• several rocks with good angles will show up better at a distance than one solitary rock, as they can be placed to complement each other;

• your arrangement should look good from all angles, inspect it from all sides and from the house before you make a final decision on the position of stones;

• imagine the rocks talking to each other, and adjust them to create more harmony between them;

• don't be too rigid, allow room for your own artistic expression.

Left: *Mirei Shigemori's use of rocks at the Matsuo Shrine in Kyoto defies the traditional naturalistic use of rocks, but still uses natural form to create a remarkable sense of drama and mystery.*

Choosing rocks & boulders

Whether you're planning a naturalistic stream garden, a Zen-influenced dry garden (*kare-sansui*) or a small Japanese-style courtyard, the care and attention you spend when selecting the rock elements will have a profound influence on the finished look and feel of the space. Rocks supply the strong yang (positive, bright and masculine) element in Japanese gardens, and larger, more sculptural pieces can be full of character. In dry gardens, they often form the main focus, so the size, shape and texture of individual rocks in a grouping is critical.

Above: *This classic trio of rocks has symbolic meanings in Japanese gardens but also works as a sculptural and harmonious arrangement.*

When selecting rocks for a Japanese garden, choose ones that you find interesting, but are not too eccentric in shape, and which can be partially buried. It is interesting to note that the rocks of the famous Ryoan-ji garden are not individually that remarkable: their hypnotic power lies in their arrangement, inspired by the way rocks and boulders can be seen poking out of the sea or a lake.

The most favoured rocks are often angular, with either pointed or flattish tops. These shapes echo the angular strokes of a paintbrush, but such distinctive shapes also stand out well when viewed from a distance. When you are using rocks as symbols – perhaps to represent Mount Horai, Shimusen or Sanzon, or crane and turtle islands, for example – make sure they are subtly arranged so that they have a quiet, still presence.

WEATHERED STONE

Stone that shows signs of weathering is particularly valued in Japanese gardens of all kinds. In these kinds of stones, a surface colonization of plants – mosses, liverworts and lichens or larger plants rooted into crevices – is of great benefit in the overall effect. This kind of natural weathering is more marked in softer, porous rock types, such as limestone and sandstone, that absorb moisture. However, you can encourage lichen growth on all types of rock by coating them with yogurt or diluted manure, and keeping them moist to get the aged effect.

It is sometimes possible to buy reclaimed stone, for example pieces from a demolished dry stone wall, either from stone merchants or architectural salvage yards. Do not, however, take a beautiful stone from the wild landscape: this is potentially damaging to the environment and individual ecosystems.

ROCKS FOR WATER FEATURES

Harder rocks like granite (a Japanese garden favourite), schist and slate tend to weather slowly, but this can be advantageous in and around water features. Sandstone and limestone are not so successful in water gardens, as porous sandstone quickly darkens with algae when wet, leaving the dry stone surround much paler, while limestone can dissolve into water, raising the pH level and adversely affecting fish.

Large, rounded boulders work very well for natural stream features since they have a water-worn quality and always combine pleasingly with cobbles and pebbles. When building cliffs and banks for a waterfall or other

Left: *Here large rounded boulders with a beautiful patina of age are set well into the ground and are surrounded by plants.*

features, ensure that the rock colours and the direction of strata of sedimentary rocks match up and look as natural as possible.

ROCKS FOR DRY GARDENS

Slate and schist shear in thin layers, producing pieces with dramatic, jagged outlines – ideal for mountainous "islands" in dry gardens. Slate may be very dark when wet with rain and is a particularly good choice for more abstract, contemplative arrangements, including black-and-white schemes. You can purchase plum- and green-toned slates, as well as more colourful kinds with reddish-brown iron deposits. Granite comes in a wide range of shades from almost white through pink and brown to almost black, and is subtly mottled and flecked. Though salts and minerals permeate many different rock types, adding colour and textural interest, it may be safer to go for more restful tones such as greys and browns, especially in a small space.

SOURCES OF NATURAL ROCK

Local garden centres are unlikely to have pieces that are the right size and shape to act as focal points, although they may have smaller rocks to choose from. Stone merchants (listed in your local telephone directory) can usually help, but for very large projects it may be advisable to visit a quarry. There you could discover pieces that have been standing for some time, distinct from the freshly quarried material, and with that all-important aged quality.

When buying by the tonne from a stone merchant or quarry, make sure you specify the rock size and quality to avoid the weight being made up with unusable rock waste. It's very important that you are at home when the stone arrives so that you can supervise the delivery process. Rough handling of rocks may damage the surface patina or cause pieces to shear off, revealing the brighter, unweathered interior, and the stone could take years to recover.

Above: *Decorative stones like these rainbow cobbles can be used sparingly as features.*

Above: *Rockery stones may be too small for Japanese gardens. Always hand select them.*

Above: *Boulders of Welsh green granite offer the perfect way of adding a rugged feel to any garden landscape.*

Do as much preparation as possible before the delivery of your rocks in the way of digging out holes or dry stream courses. You may also need to hire a bulldozer or digger to lift heavy stones into their sockets; alternatively you can use a block-and-tackle pulley system. Ensure that the new rocks are well protected and cushioned to prevent any possible damage caused by cables during lifting.

Above: *The markings on these gneiss boulders are more subtle, making them easier to place.*

Above: *Smooth, sea-worn boulders have a pleasing texture and work well with cobbles.*

Above: *You would be advised to use thicker pieces of slate for stepping stones, as thin pieces tend to crack under any pressure.*

MANMADE ALTERNATIVES

Where access to a garden is restricted or weight is an issue, for example on load-bearing surfaces such as roofs and balconies, use resin or fibreglass rocks and boulders instead. These are hollow and easy to lift but can look very realistic when bedded in and surrounded by plants and perhaps a few cobbles. You can buy them on-line or from landscaping exhibitions.

Moving rocks & boulders

Stones and rocks can vary enormously in weight, size and shape. Your choice of rocks may be determined by your budget, and also by how they can be manoeuvred into place. In a small garden, or behind a house with only a narrow gated entrance, you may have problems in getting the rocks into position. In more open spaces there will be no such limitation, but you should still consider the weight and potential unwieldiness of large pieces and be prepared to hire professionals to move them. If moving smaller rocks, take great care with your back.

Above: *Mount Horai is the tallest of the mythical Mystic Isles, often portrayed by the tallest rock. Moving such large rocks into position requires careful thought and planning, and the right equipment.*

MOVING SMALL ROCKS WITH A BAR

You will need
- two people to carry the rock
- strong straps (from a hire shop)
- a scaffolding pole and shackle

1 If a rock is the right size for strapping, wrap the two loose ends of the strap around a scaffolding pole, securing them with a shackle.

2 Ensure the length of strap is equal to a little less than the height to the carriers' shoulders. This will mean that the rock only need be lifted off the ground a short way, just enough to move it. It will also be safer if the rock is hung as close to the ground as possible, in case it should fall out of the straps.

3 One person at either end of the pole can lift the pole on to their shoulders, and then the two people can lift and move the rock.

MOVING SMALL TO MEDIUM ROCKS WITH A SACK TRUCK

You will need
- a sack truck, preferably with pneumatic tyres as this will make it easier to pull over soft ground – hard wheels will easily get bogged down, even in gravel

1 Lift up one end of the rock until it stands on end and slide the sack truck as close up to the rock as you can.

2 Roll the rock over on to the plate of the sack truck. You may be able to slide the plate under the rock without having to roll the rock by lifting one end a little bit off the ground.

3 Place one foot against the axle of the truck as you pull the handle back. Small rocks are easy to move around like this with the handle at around 45 degrees. It is easier to pull than to push.

NARROW ENTRANCES

If the garden has a narrow entrance, a sack truck is useful to move smaller stones. For larger stones, you may need to hire a crane to lift the rocks over the house. Although expensive, cranes will carry a lot more weight.

MOVING ROCKS WITH A SKID LOADER

You will need
- a hired skid loader
- medium-size rocks

1 You may be able to drive the bucket under the rock without having to move the rock.

2 Otherwise, either prop up one end of the rock using a post or a crow-bar while the bucket slides underneath, or, with help if the rock is too large, roll the rock into the bucket.

SELECTING THE BEST METHOD

The size of rocks you need to move will dictate the method you use:

- to move rocks by hand, they must be small but you can control positioning;

- a sack truck will carry small–medium rocks, and will fit through narrow gaps;

- a skid loader can be used to transport medium rocks, and the weight is taken by the equipment;

- a mini-digger or foreloader can move rocks up to its weight limit.

MOVING MEDIUM TO LARGE ROCKS WITH A MINI-DIGGER OR FORELOADER

You will need
- a mini-digger or foreloader on a tractor, or back-hoe, plus a skilled licensed driver
- hard hats, steel toe-capped boots and gloves
- a block of wood or fencing post
- lifting straps with looped ends – these can be hired, and are classified according to the weight they are designed to carry. Go for heavier straps than you think you will need.
- U-shaped shackles to bind the ends of the straps

1 If the rock is lying flat, prop up the top end in order to slide the straps underneath. Use the digger to lift up one end and slide a block of wood underneath to prop it up.

2 Wind the straps two or three times around the rock at approximately a third of the way from the top. This position should keep the rock secure when the straps tighten around it. Tighten the two ends by pushing one end through the loop at the other end. Make the two ends with equal length to spare and ensure they end up at either side of the rock. This will allow it to hang more vertically when you lift it up.

3 Wind the two loose ends around a secure point on the lifting bucket, and bring the two loops close enough to each other to be secured together. Using a suitable shackle, clamp the two loops together.

4 Lift the machine loader bucket up until the straps are tense and lift the bucket gently and slowly until you can see how the rock will hang from the bucket.

5 It may take two or three attempts until the straps are secure and the rock is hanging so that it can be manipulated into place.

SAFETY NOTE

Before moving the rock, ensure that it is hanging securely and that everyone is at a safe distance.

Paving & stepping stones

Paving is another important element of a Japanese garden. Pathways through the Japanese garden can be made of different kinds of stone, from new or manmade paving stones to reclaimed stone from various sources. Stepping stones are often used in water features or gravel areas. Straight lines and right angles are usually best avoided, as curves and natural forms complement the concept and style of a Japanese garden better. If care is taken at the planning stage, the final result can look completely natural and spontaneous.

RANDOM PAVING

This kind of paving, using irregularly cut stone pieces, is popular in Japanese gardens. The stone is generally bought by the tonne and needs careful laying to accommodate pieces of varying thickness and to minimize the width of mortar joints. Random stone can be laid as a pathway "filler" in conjunction with straight-edged, rectangular pieces and adjacent to sections of geometric patterning, for example next to pavers set as a line of diamonds. Kerbstones and stone setts are also used to define pathways and to separate areas of differing colour, pattern or function.

RECLAIMED STONES

Paving that is reclaimed, with a rough-hewn look or with worn or weathered surfaces is much sought after. Japanese gardeners will often incorporate pieces once used for other purposes, including original millstones, old gateposts and worn stone door lintels or steps. A good source of reclaimed stones is architectural salvage yards.

STEPPING STONES

A very common feature of Japanese gardens, stepping stones are used in both wet and dry locations. A zigzagging pathway might artfully combine rounded stepping stones with rectangular elements, often also mingled with cobbles or pebbles. Handcrafted granite stepping stones, broadly circular and with softly bevelled edges, are laid following age-old patterns.

Whatever the location – crossing a pool, a mossy woodland floor or in a gravel area – the stones are always set slightly proud of the surrounding surface. Stepping stones should be well bedded into the substrate to give the path stability and also to create a

Left: *Weathered stone slabs covered with mosses and lichens are used here as stepping stones in a sea of pebbles. Note how they are set proud of their surroundings. Rectangular pieces are often mixed with irregular ones.*

Above: *Granite setts are rough hewn and therefore more suitable for Japanese gardens where natural-looking materials are preferred.*

"rooted" quality. This means that individual stones are likely to need a depth of at least 15cm (6in).

TYPES OF NATURAL STONE FOR PAVING

Certain types of sedimentary rock can be split very easily along the overlying layers, making them ideal contenders for paving. These include pale grey or creamy coloured limestone, which often has visible remnants of fossilized organisms and shells. Sandstones, such as buff-coloured York stone paving and millstone grit in Britain, and flagstone and bluestone in the US, are also used for paving. Good-quality reclaimed York stone commands a high price, but nowadays imported Indian sandstone can be more economical and just as effective. It ranges in colour from almost black to buff with pink or yellow tinting. If possible, look at samples of the different colour types laid as paving, both dry and wetted, before making your selection, as the colour may change dramatically when the stone is wet, perhaps making it not the perfect choice after all.

Indian sandstone is widely available in a wide range of sizes, and is hand cut to leave a bevelled, rough-cut edge

Above: *Indian sandstone comes in a wide range of colours.*

Above: *York stone paving slabs covered with lichen and moss.*

Above: *Limestone is a sedimentary rock that gives an aged patina to paving.*

Above: *Traditional granite stepping stones are usually rounded or irregular in shape.*

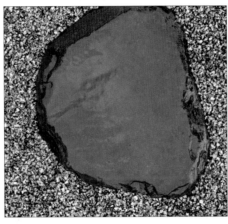

Above: *Slate stepping stones look wonderfully glossy and dark after rain.*

Above: *Used sparingly, stepping stones with imprinted symbols or patterns can add interest.*

with a more rustic appearance than diamond- or machine-cut stone. There are, however, some practices to do with the labour and sourcing of Indian sandstone that mean that this material is not guaranteed to be ethically sourced, so you might want to look for alternatives until better standards are established.

When buying any regular-cut stone, buy by the square metre/yard rather than by the tonne, and specify a minimum and maximum thickness.

Granite is traditional in Japanese gardens. As it is one of the most resistant stones to wear and tear, it is much sought after, especially when the surface shows signs of erosion, as this signifies great age. In shady or damp paved areas, granite and other non-porous rock types have an advantage over limestone and sandstone because, with the more porous stone, moisture absorption leads to the growth of slippery algae, which must be removed periodically for safety. This does not apply to granite, which is less absorbent. Choose hand-finished granite paving or tumbled granite setts for a natural effect.

Slate is another excellent paving option, although pieces tend to be cut relatively thinly, so they must be laid on a full mortar bed to give adequate support. Check before buying imported slate to ensure that the pieces are thick enough for external use and that they are of outdoor quality, meaning that they won't shatter or flake on exposure to the elements.

MANMADE ALTERNATIVES

Manufacturers of concrete paving now produce very convincing stone reproductions using old stone pavers as moulds to give a natural-looking effect. But these products can wear and chip, then exposing the concrete interior, and the slabs tend not to be as thick as natural stone. However, driveway setts (small blocks) are a good option for paving close to buildings and in more formal areas.

If used with care, poured concrete can be an effective and inexpensive material for making large stepping stones or areas resembling exposed bedrock. The mix is poured into a mould of sufficient depth to prevent cracking, using curved shuttering. Before it completely hardens, it is textured with a wetted nylon hand brush and various tools. Alternatively, you can add pebbles and shingle to the concrete to create an interestingly textured surface, then use a soft brush and watering can to expose some areas, thus mirroring the processes of natural erosion.

Cobbles, pebbles & paddlestones

Often used for pathways, in open areas or by water features, the smooth, rounded surfaces of cobbles, pebbles and paddlestones make a pleasing contrast to rough-surfaced regular paving slabs or flat stepping stones. They can be a wonderful foil for plants, especially those with linear or strap-like foliage. Different schemes call for different sizes and types of pebbles or cobbles, in keeping with the scale and nature of the garden. Remember that the beauty of the stone may be revealed only when wet, so when you are buying stones ask to see samples in and out of water.

Above: *Graded pebbles camouflage the edge of a butyl-lined pond or stream, creating a beach or natural stream bank effect.*

COBBLES

Acting as a helpful transition from large rounded boulders to smaller pebbles, cobbles tend to be required in relatively small quantities for ordinary domestic garden schemes.

In fact, in a compact urban space such as an enclosed courtyard or roof garden, you may need only a handful, which is just as well because they tend to be sold individually and can be quite expensive.

Some cobbles are relatively unmarked but range in colour from white, through brown, red and grey to almost black, reflecting different rock types. Paler greys and browns may also show attractive banding, for which you will pay a premium. When hand-selecting small numbers of stones, look carefully to ensure that they are the colour, shape and texture you want, as cobbles are sometimes split or damaged in transit.

Large cobbles of the sort originally used to surface the roads and stable yards of old are sometimes available from reclamation yards. Bigger garden centres often have a few large cobbles for sale, stored in crates or on palettes. Cobbles may be commercially dredged from the sea bottom or taken from gravel pits. For larger quantities, visit your local stone merchant or a gravel pit if there's one in your area. You can't just go to the beach and help yourself, though – laws normally prohibit the removal of cobbles or pebbles from a beach or the bank of a stream.

Left: *It is important to place larger stones and cobbles by hand to create a naturalistic effect. Here there is the impression of a stream trickling down into a larger, deeper pool. The cobbles are graded by size and infilled with gravel.*

PEBBLES

In nature, pebbles often represent a wide mixture of rock types, fragments of which have been worn smooth and rounded by the action of water or ice. When wet, they glisten and may show an extraordinary range of colours, flecks and stripes. Suppliers normally have samples in buckets for you to examine. Pebbles may also be colour selected so that, as well as the natural mixed shades, you can buy pure white or jet black for special projects.

In small quantities, pebbles are sold in bags or sacks, but they are extremely heavy – the average car could safely transport only three or four bags at a time. You can also buy them bagged or loose by the tonne delivered from stone merchants. Pebbles are graded and sold by size – you'll normally find at least two or three sizes at larger garden centres.

MIXING COBBLES AND PEBBLES

Sometimes cobbles and pebbles are used together in Japanese gardens to create a pleasingly natural look. When you are using these stones as ground cover, mix cobbles and pebbles of different sizes. If you want to create a beach effect at the margin of a butyl-lined pond, or in a dry stream bed, lay cobbles, pebbles and shingle in graded bands and curving sections, reflecting the strata formed by water in nature. Check that the various types you have in mind are compatible in terms of colour and texture. If you intend to use cobbles and pebbles in and around your pond or by a stream, check that they are fish friendly and wash them thoroughly before use to avoid contaminating the water.

PADDLESTONES

These flat or paddle-shaped pieces of stone with gently rounded edges come in sizes from 15cm (6in) across to as much as 60cm (24in). Although they are sometimes used for ground cover and for creating interesting surface textures, these stones are ideal for representing a stream because the pieces can be laid to

overlap and "flow" in the direction of the imaginary water. They can also be used to suggest the rippled surface of a pool or, on a much larger and more ambitious scale, a lake or even a sea. Paddlestones have a markedly different look to cobbles and pebbles and are therefore best laid with some visual barrier to separate them from these more rounded, glossy aggregates.

Above: *You can buy pebbles graded by size bagged or loose from builders' merchants.*

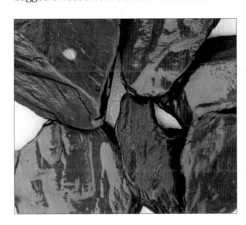

Above: *Slate pebbles eroded by the action of water are softer looking than chippings.*

Above: *These red marble pebbles have been set into cement to create a textured surface.*

PREPARING THE GROUND

Do not lay cobbles, pebbles and paddlestones directly on to soil, because this is likely to contain perennial weed roots and annual weed seeds. Instead use a black horticultural or landscape membrane, which will allow water to pass through but which prevents soil and weeds from coming to the surface.

Above: *Ask to see pebbles wet before you buy as they can look quite different.*

Above: *Paddlestones are characterized by their large, flat, broadly oval shapes.*

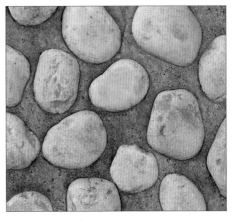

Above: *White marble pebbles are sometimes used for more stylized designs.*

Sand, grit, gravel & slate

A feeling of space is very important in Japanese gardens, and open sand or gravel areas help to keep the structure of the garden simple and are easy to maintain if laid carefully. Sand or grit can be raked into patterns, as in a traditional Zen garden, and although gravel cannot be raked into quite such well-defined designs, it makes an interesting and subtly coloured backdrop to a large rock or boulder. Whichever kind of ground cover you choose, make sure that the preparation is meticulous and you will be rewarded with a natural-looking, easy-to-keep area.

Above: *Pieces of natural stone here form an informal pathway. Clay tiles have been used to separate the two types of gravel.*

SAND AND FINE GRIT

A well-known feature of many Japanese gardens is an area of sand or fine grit, raked into swirling patterns to represent forms in nature. (See overleaf for some examples.) This can be a practical option for a newly created Japanese garden if thought is given to the materials, the size of the area and its location within the garden. In dry gardens, the patterns represent the movement of water. More abstractly, in the Zen tradition, these raked sand or gravel patterns can also represent the tranquil mind.

The best location for this effect is in a sheltered garden or courtyard. The fine material traditionally used is not suitable for very open, windy locations as the patterns will be disturbed too quickly. After periods of heavy rainfall or strong winds, you may well find that designs need to be re-raked or brushed quite frequently.

A number of grades and colours of sand and grit can be used to create your design. In bright, sunny locations, and especially for larger areas, avoid pure white sand, as this can create an uncomfortable glare – darker shades are more tranquil. However, paler coloured sands can bring light into a shaded passageway or courtyard area, or an enclosed space that is viewed through a window.

Prepare the area by separating the sand and base material from the underlying soil using landscape membrane. Make sure that you keep the sand or grit well away from areas of lawn as it can damage mower blades.

COARSE GRIT AND GRAVEL

Gravel is a relatively inexpensive ground cover when compared to paving. When laid over landscape membrane, it can also be surprisingly low maintenance. Finer gravels may be used as an alternative surface around rock formations in a dry Zen garden, though they won't allow for intricately raked patterns.

You can buy gravel in a range of grades. The coarser types (up to 2cm/¾in across) are best for walking on, especially if the area is close to the house, because they don't get caught in the treads of shoes and tend to bed down well and stay put. You should try to avoid using fine grit and gravel under trees, as it will be difficult to clear fallen leaves in the autumn. However, you can use a leaf blower on larger diameter gravels and pebbles without disturbing them.

Finer gravel can be kicked about by foot traffic and all too easily makes a seed bed for weeds, so it will need more maintenance than the coarser varieties.

For water gardens, you will find that river gravels and beach shingles give a natural look, being composed of rounded, water-worn pieces that glisten when wet. They normally come in a combination of browns and greys – soft, neutral colours that work well in restful Japanese gardens and also

Above: *Where fine sand is used, be prepared for regular maintenance, even in sheltered areas.*

Above: *Gravel is often used as a representation of water in the Japanese garden.*

combine nicely with pebbles and cobbles (see pages 74–75). Avoid golden-coloured gravels or coloured chippings, which tend not to look very natural.

DIFFERENT SOURCES

To purchase sand or grit for raking, you may need to contact a specialist Japanese garden supplier as it is not easy to find the right grade or colour in ordinary garden centres, stone merchants or builders' merchants. The type of grit used in Japan is made from degraded rock fragments that measure about 3mm (⅛in) in diameter. However, certain types of horticultural grit may make an acceptable alternative if you cannot find it.

Though bagged gravel is readily available from garden centres, you can buy it more economically from builders' merchants. Having bags or truckloads delivered will also avoid unwanted wear and tear to your car. In this case, tell the supplier what area you plan to cover and to what depth and they will calculate exactly how much to deliver.

OTHER GROUND COVER

Stone chippings of hard rocks such as granite are also suitable for ground cover, and they come in a wider range of colours than gravel, including black, shades of grey, plum, green, brownish-red and white. You can purchase a range of grades. Whatever colour you choose, make sure that it blends with or makes a suitable contrast to the type of rock you are using as a central feature. In general, chippings, with their jagged, sharp edges, tend to work better in a dry garden setting than in a water garden. In a water garden you would expect the natural substrate to be smooth and water-worn rather than spiky and frost-shattered.

Slate waste is now widely available in garden centres as an alternative surfacing material to gravel for paths and open areas. The flat shards bed down well and don't tend to get kicked about like fine gravel. This material is also resistant to weed growth, although like the other ground cover materials it benefits from being laid on a horticultural or landscape membrane. Slate is usually sold in bags, and comes in dark grey, or with plum or green tones.

Larger pieces of slate can be laid like paddlestones to create the effect of flowing water in a dry stream feature, and finer grades can be applied as a mulch around plants or to create the illusion of a body of still water in a dry garden. Fine slate works well to make a dry "pool" crossed by an arched bridge or stepping stones, or at the base of a stone waterfall.

Above: *These 5mm (¼in) diameter granite chippings are ideal for traditional-style gardens.*

Above: *Pearly quartz chippings can be used to lighten shady courtyards.*

Above: *Blue slate "waste" is readily available and useful for creating dry pools and streams.*

Above: *Dark-coloured Welsh granite chippings could be used to contrast with pale cobbles.*

Above: *Always lay chippings over permeable landscape membrane to limit weed problems.*

Above: *Use coloured or pale granite chippings sparingly in more naturalistic settings.*

CHOOSING SAND OR GRAVEL

The sand or gravel can be 3–10mm (⅛–⅜in) in diameter. If it is too fine, it will get blown about and will not rake well into patterns, although in the famous garden of Shisendo, in Kyoto, the sand is very fine and is brushed with a twig broom into delicate patterns rather than raked. The ideal size is 4–6mm (³⁄₁₆in) in diameter. A mixture of sizes and a degree of roughness will help the stones in the ridges to bind with one another. If they are too round and smooth, the stones tend to roll and the ridges flatten out too readily.

The sand can be laid over a concrete base, but it is important to ensure that the whole site is well drained. An alternative would be a firm but open base of hardcore overlaid with rough stone and sand mix (known as hoggin or scalpings) in order to allow the surface to drain.

The most sought-after gravel in Kyoto is made of a silvery-grey granite and quartz grit. It is very precious, very expensive and becoming quite difficult to obtain, even in Japan. In other countries it may be difficult to find the ideal kind of gravel or sand, though situations will vary. Avoid white marble chips, as these will be

Above: *With the right type of fine gravel, you can create a range of clearly defined patterns.*

Below: *In the temple garden of Tofuku-ji, "waves" of gravel have been raked into abstractions. The main set of lines runs parallel throughout the garden while those closest to the edge curve to meet it.*

USING GRAVEL: KEY ELEMENTS

Finding the right site Gravel "pools" of water should always be laid on a level site. Don't try to make them on even a gentle slope.

Colour of gravel Don't use gravel that is bright white as this will glare in bright sunshine; try to find a colour that is light enough to feel like water and to show up in moonlight.

Size of gravel Gravel size can be as small as 3mm (⅛in) and up to 10mm (⅜in) in diameter, depending on the kind of pattern you want to make and the area to be covered. The ideal size for raked gravel is 4–6mm (³⁄₁₆in). If the gravel is too small and smooth it will collapse too readily.

Depth of gravel Gravel should be laid to a depth of about 5cm (2in) to give enough material to rake.

RAKING PATTERNS: KEY ELEMENTS

Raking without leaving footprints
Simply start in the middle of the "canvas" and work outwards.

Making a satisfying and authentic pattern The bulk of your space should be empty and raked in parallel lines. In the most famous dry garden in the world, the Ryoan-ji, the lines are all parallel except the concentric waves that lap around each of the 15 rocks.

Keeping it simple Avoid making too much of the space busy with too many different and elaborate patterns as this will defeat the calming influence of the water effect. Simple is best.

Imitating the flow of water Around rocks and plants, you can rake as if the waves were lapping against their shores. In other places you can "draw" whirlpools, waving patterns, or patterns that imitate the variable flow in rivers (always remembering that your overall pattern should be simple). Dry streams made of gravel can also be raked to imitate the flow of small brooks.

Stream current

Stylized wave

Ocean wave

Surf pattern

Brook

Stylized ocean wave

Concentric ocean wave

Combination: whirlpool and stream current

Concentric ripples

Whirlpool

Elliptical concentric ripple

far too bright and look a bit funereal. Darker colours can be used but they will tend to look more like muddy water than the reflective purity that is so ideal in these gardens.

If you would prefer not to commit yourself to frequent raking, then any kind of gravel that is not too chunky would do; however, even in this case you will need to rake it from time to time to keep it looking clean and tidy. If you like the raking process, you could make it a regular practice. How frequently you need to rake a dry garden will depend on the degree to which the patterns get disturbed by heavy rains, wind, birds and small animals, or in autumn by how many leaves fall on them. Before you re-do the raking, level out the whole site

with a broom, a board or the flat side of a hay rake, so that you are working on a blank canvas.

SAND AND GRAVEL PATTERNS

In Zen temples, dry gardens often have areas of sand or gravel raked into elaborate patterns. These are simple abstract imitations of the movement of waves on water. The simplicity and rhythm are also symbolic of the spiritual life. They create a sense of space and wonder, helping the mind to enter a state of contemplation and quiet – one of the goals of Zen Buddhism. The raking of the sand is part of the spiritual practice of Zen monks, who enter a state of "no-mind"

as they walk backwards, drawing their rake and pulling the sand into ridges and troughs.

The traditional patterns made by the monks are a closely guarded secret. If you enjoy the effect of these dry gardens but are less interested in the high goals of Zen meditation, simply imagine that you are "painting" a sea in sand. The sand can be the wide open sea or a river; it also represents the white "canvas" background of a landscape painting. Knowing this can open up numerous possibilities for abstract patterns, but keep the overall pattern simple or you will distract the mind of the viewer, rather than soothing it into a state of calm.

Dry water

The original dry landscape gardens focused on the placement of rocks in moss or grass. In later dry gardens, rocks were set in sand, gravel and among pebbles, with these elements arranged and spread to imitate the qualities of water: either as a stream, when on a flat surface, or as a waterfall, when carefully constructed on a slope (see pages 92–93). The important concept with a dry waterfall is to have high stones at the back of the design to represent the waterfall height. It can then end in a dry stream or pond when it reaches the foot of the slope.

Above: *At Tofukuji, in Kyoto, the 20th-century artist-designer Mirei Shigemori used sand to imitate water, recalling ocean waves lapping at island shores.*

DRY STREAMS: KEY ELEMENTS

Assessing the slope A dry stream can be built down a gentle slope. On a steeper slope you will need to create a series of dry falls, or alternatively make the stream take a wandering course.

Making a meandering dry stream You can use the same principles as for a meandering water stream (see pages 98–101), on a flattish site with a wider expanse of stones.

Paths and bridges Design paths that can cross over the stream or that look as though they can, so that you can build a slab stone bridge across the stream. Bridges will add to the illusion of a real stream.

Adding waterfalls Small "falls" can be built into the stream to make it look more realistic.

Exaggerating the effect Remember that you are suggesting a stream rather than making an exact copy, so the effect should ideally look as artistic as it is naturalistic. If it is too naturalistic, the stream will simply look as though the water has run dry.

Planting Place clumps of plants that have a "wet" look on the sides of the stream, for example sedges, hostas or tricyrtis.

ROCKS AND PEBBLES

The first two great gardens with rocks set in moss or grass were the 14th-century Saiho-ji, or Moss Temple, and Tenryu-ji. At the latter there is a superb dry waterfall, known as the Dragon Gate Waterfall, created with all the power of a real waterfall. At the Saiho-ji, there is a large turtle representation and a hillside with dramatic arrangements of rocks. The

Below: *This dry garden at St Mawgan in Cornwall shows the same kind of enterprising spirit seen in many of Shigemori's designs. The effect is like that of a flooded inland river basin.*

Zen monks who created such dry gardens realized that the imagination is more captivated by a suggestion than by reality. Or, as they might have put it, the power of the imagined shape yields a far greater truth than one locked up in the real. This is what is meant by the poetic term *yugen*, or "the spirit of hidden depth".

Streams, as opposed to still water, are portrayed in their "dry" form by the use of river-washed pebbles laid out carefully in overlapping patterns to indicate a sense of flow. The image is completed by the use of a few larger boulders or rocks, as well as bridges made of large stone slabs.

MODERN INTERPRETATIONS

There is great design potential for contemporary designers to use a dry rock-and-sand garden to create even more abstract patterns, using quarry-blasted rocks rather than naturally occurring weathered stones. This takes the "suggestive" nature of the dry landscape into the realm of contemporary design. If you are careful with the composition, space and balance of the layout, these gardens can be very successful, as well as fairly easy to manage. Not all modern Japanese garden designers follow Zen precepts; they have become more Western in outlook. However, the overall design of these modern gardens remains essentially Japanese.

Above: *This dry garden at the Brunei Gallery roof garden in London can be interpreted as a river with large natural boulders being crossed by a staggered carved stone bridge that stretches from bank to bank.*

Below: *A dry waterfall in Kew Gardens shows a carp stone placed at the base of the waterfall. This symbolizes the striving of the individual to rise above himself. A carp who reaches the top of the waterfall is transformed into a dragon.*

DRY WATERFALLS: KEY ELEMENTS

Using a flat site In a flat, rectangular courtyard setting, a dry waterfall can be set into one corner.

Using a hilly site In a natural setting, a dry waterfall should be built into the side of a hill or a steep slope to look effective.

Exaggerating the effect Good dry waterfalls should have a "monumental" feel to look impressive, as if a lot of water fell down them at one time. Don't be afraid to exaggerate this effect. Some versions use very large rocks.

Choosing the top stones Find some flat-topped stones for the points at which the water would have flowed over the waterfall. The top stone should always have two larger stones on either side of it. For a simple arrangement, these three stones might be enough.

Imagining the water Always imagine the flow of the waterfall as if it had real water in it. This will help you decide how to lay the stones.

Making pools Some waterfalls have small pools halfway down them. In a dry waterfall these are filled with gravel to imitate the standing water.

Making a dry waterfall & stream

Waterfalls in Japanese gardens can be real sources of water, or they can alternatively be dry cascades (*kare taki*) in which stones simply suggest the movement of a waterfall. *Kare taki* exist in various forms, ranging from a single cascade to a more complex one of multiple stages. Each one is documented in Japan's earliest known manual of gardening, the *Sakuteiki*, which describes ten different forms of waterfall construction, stipulates the proper height and width of a cascade, and advises the reader on the appropriate types of stones to use for such a feature.

This dry cascade is suitable for a garden with a natural slope, and uses a plastic liner and a stepped selection of rocks from the top to the base. Such a dry waterfall is seen as highly symbolic by Japanese garden masters, and the aesthetic positioning of rocks, often in groups of three, is key. The dry waterfall forms part of a dry landscape, which might also include evergreen trees and shrubs, moss and raked sand, which symbolizes streaming water. Here the dry stream at the bottom is represented by gravel and more well-positioned rocks.

Above: *Dry waterfalls are often built on a series of levels, so that the gravel that imitates the water can be held in the "pools" as the dry cascade descends down the slope.*

Opposite: *Sedges and ferns tucked around the rocks recall the plants that you might find alongside a mountain stream.*

You will need
- 2 people to move the stones
- a large backing stone
- 2 side stones
- various other large stones and boulders
- concrete
- plastic sheeting
- gravel
- a long base stone to represent a bridge
- a shovel

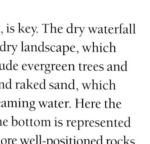

1 Prepare the location by digging over the land following the shape of the proposed waterfall and stream. Then dig a hole to fit the backing stone and manoeuvre the stone into position.

2 Set the backing stone and pack the soil around it tightly so that it remains steady. Larger stones and boulders should be set in the hole with concrete to ensure they remain solidly in place.

3 Having achieved the basic stepping-stone shape from backing stone to lower level stone, prepare the ground to accommodate two side stones.

4 Place stones to form a pool structure, as shown here, that is positioned directly below the four key waterfall stones.

5 For the dry stream, prepare the land beneath the pool. The stream should appear on a lower level again to maintain the illusion of falling water.

6 Position further stones to frame the shape of the stream, judging their positions as you go.

7 Having completed your stone structure, cut plastic sheeting to line each of the enclosed areas. This ensures that plants will not grow into the gravel.

8 Shovel gravel on top of the plastic sheeting to cover it fully. Ensure that the gravel layer representing the stream is at least 2.5cm (1in) thick.

9 As a finishing touch, position another long, flat stone across the two base stones around the stream to represent a bridge.

Plants & planting

The "hard" elements of a garden – gravel, rocks and architectural features – are important in Japanese garden design. However, "soft" elements – plants, trees and shrubs – are also vital. Many people regard Japanese gardens as making little use of plants, and while it is true that they are often less central than in, for example, a traditional English cottage garden, many Japanese gardens use a great range of plants. The crucial point is that the plants are always subservient to the overall design, and will be carefully placed and managed to this end.

Above: *On the west coast of Europe, near the sea, there is enough moisture in the air for moss to grow on the ground and over the trees.*

GROUND COVER

An important ingredient in most Japanese gardens for ground cover, moss requires the right balance of sun and shade to grow well. In Kyoto, for example, it will grow virtually anywhere because of the high rainfall during the summer. The variety of different species of moss gives the surface of the garden a beautiful velvety texture in all shades of green, often highlighted by the dappled sun if the moss is growing beneath trees. By contrast, the popular Western ground cover of grass is not widely used in Japanese gardens. The advantage of growing moss rather than grass is that it gives the Japanese designer much more freedom in terms of positioning plants, as it does not need to be mown in the same way as grass. It does, however, need to be cared for and weeded to keep it in shape. Rocks can also be positioned without the constraints placed on gardens in which grass is the main foundation. If you are not blessed with a climate in which moss grows freely, you can easily improvise by using a ground cover of mondo grass (*Ophiopogon*) or perhaps instead some shorn bamboos.

Below: *It is important to have the right amount of light and shade to maintain the moss cover. Too much sun and it burns out; too little and it dies out. Many species of moss have combined to knit this carpet at Sanzen-in.*

Below: *This uneven chequerboard of stone squares sunk into a sea of moss and edged with roof tiles is at the garden of Tofuku-ji; this garden harmonizes the natural, the architectural and the contemporary.*

Grass is rarely used as ground cover in the Japanese garden except in very large gardens, where drought-resistant zoyza grass can be planted. This deep-rooting grass is not mown tight to the ground, and should be left at a height of approximately 8cm (3in), which gives a dense, cushiony turf. However, this grass does turn brown in the winter. Grass on banks and between rocks in Japanese gardens should be trimmed and clipped as neatly as in a Western garden.

SYMBOLIC PLANTS

While plants are not used as much as in Western gardens, when they are used they are not simply a design element but often hold symbolic significance too. So most Japanese gardens will contain one or more of the most symbolic plants, such as plum, cherry, bamboo, pine or maple. The Japanese plum (*Prunus mume*) is a symbol of purity and hope; the cherry (*Prunus serrulata*) with its short-lived blossom reminds us of our mortality, while the Japanese maple (*Acer palmatum*) is a symbol of longevity.

JAPAN'S NATURAL FLORA

Although Japan's mountains, streams and coastlines are brimming with superb flora, the disciplined restraint of Japanese gardens focuses on certain types of plants. The native plant area in Kyoto's botanical garden is full of plants that Western gardeners would relish, but most of them would not find a home in a Japanese garden.

The problem with many Western imitations of Japanese gardens is that designers cannot resist using attractive Japanese plants that would not normally be chosen by a Japanese designer – for example, those that are considered too colourful or are the wrong shape. However, this restraint does not mean that the Japanese do not appreciate plants. On the contrary, the Japanese celebrate flowers perhaps more than any other nation, especially flowers that signify seasonal change or are associated with certain festivals.

SEASONAL VARIETY

As the last snows melt in spring, the plum trees (or Japanese apricots) start wafting out their scent and are appreciated with a quiet reverence. The cherry blossom season then attracts thousands to gardens with the best displays, with parties gathering under their boughs. Although there are a number of native shrubs that flower in late spring – some deutzias, spiraeas and kerrias – they are considered as secondary to the cherries, wisterias, peonies, azaleas and camellias.

The summer begins with a show of irises that grow in swampy ground at the heads of ponds, and in pots as prized and cosseted specimens. Hollyhocks (*Alcea rosea*), hydrangeas, the lotus (*Nelumbo*) and the morning glory (*Ipomoea*) are all cultivated to keep the season going as long as possible. Many plants originating in different climates do not grow well in the hot, wet Japanese summers, but will revive in the spring and autumn.

In autumn Japanese maples are just as important as the spring cherries in the Japanese calendar. Their fiery reds contrast with the deep greens of the evergreen pines and the fleeting blossom of the autumn-flowering camellia (*Camellia sasanqua*). Bush clover, balloon flower, toad lilies and *Farfugium* all add extra interest.

The most favoured plants for winter interest are bamboos and pines, and these can withstand the cold impressively. Snow-covered pines make a beautiful sight. Japan is also blessed with an exceptional number of evergreen shrubs that thrive in its acidic soil and temperate climate.

PLANTING STYLES

Most shrubs in the Japanese garden are set out in random, natural-looking groups or as individual specimens. Formal, symmetrical styles are rarely used, and shrubs and flowers are not planted for their textures or colours.

Below: *A pathway through the bamboo garden at the Hakone Gardens in Saratoga, California. This part of the garden contains many highly prized types of bamboo, including a black-stemmed variety.*

In tea gardens, you will find plants such as ferns that lend a wild quality to the design. In stark contrast, other gardens are planted with clipped evergreens, a look at its most artistic in the 17th-century art of *o-karikomi*, in which groups of shrubs, usually azaleas and camellias, are clipped into abstract topiary shapes (see pages 98–101). Hedges are another important feature for which a great miscellany of shrubs can be used. While some hedges look fairly uniform from a distance, they may actually contain as many as 20 or more genera from a list including *Elaeagnus, Pieris, Camellia, Rhododendron, Ficus, Aucuba, Osmanthus* and *Nandina*.

The Japanese garden is by no means devoid of colour and scent. Town gardens might include hydrangeas, hollyhocks, sweet peas (*Lathyrus odoratus*), morning glories and clematis or azaleas growing in pots outside the door. This planting effect is something that would be simple to recreate in any small city garden. The pots themselves can be in all shapes and sizes but in Japan are often quite small. The compost (soil mix) would be annually renewed to ensure a good supply of nutrients.

Above: *A dwarf Japanese red pine creates a much softer look than the harsher and more rugged black pine.*

PLANTS THROUGH THE SEASONS

Spring
Plum blossom (*Prunus mume*)
Cherry blossom (*Sakura*)
Deutzia
Spiraea
Japanese rose (*Kerria*)
Wisteria
Peony (*Paeonia*)
Azalea
Camellia

Summer
Iris
Hollyhock (*Alcea rosea*)
Hydrangea
Lotus blossom (*Nelumbo*)
Morning glory (*Ipomoea*)

Autumn
Japanese maple (*Acer*)
Evergreen pines
Autumn-flowering camellia (*Camellia sasanqua*)
Bush clover (*Lespedeza*)
Balloon flower (*Platycodon*)
Toad lily (*Tricyrtis*)
Farfugium

Winter
Bamboos
Evergreen pines and other shrubs

PLANTING TECHNIQUE

Although you can plant pot-grown plants at almost any time of year, you may need to water them more frequently if you plant in late spring or summer. The ideal time of year for planting is autumn but if your chosen plant is tender, especially when young and small, it would be better to wait until the late winter or early spring. It is not a good idea to attempt to plant anything when the ground is very hard and dry, very wet and boggy, or when it is frozen solid.

The standard planting technique shown below should be adapted around the different types and sizes of plant available as well as around the type of roots the plant has. Before you start the process of planting, you will need to be prepared with a garden spade and fork, some well-rotted manure, a rake and a watering can.

Right: *Take care when planting some species of bamboo as they can be invasive. Root barriers can be placed in a circle around the plant to prevent it from invading the garden.*

1 Place the plant, still in its pot, where you want to plant it and mark around the spot with your spade or place a cane. Then put the plant to one side, digging a hole 50 per cent wider than the pot and 5–7.5cm (2–3in) deeper. Break up the soil in the bottom of the hole and replace it.

2 While holding the pot, turn it over. Squeeze the sides gently with the hand holding the base of the pot and ease it off with the same hand. If it doesn't come off readily, give the rim a firm tap on something hard and check that no roots have emerged through the holes in the pot and are holding the plant in.

3 Before planting, check that the hole is the correct depth – normally, the same as it was in the pot. In very heavy soil, planting slightly higher would help to avoid waterlogging, and in light soil you could plant deeper to increase the water supply. Add one or two forkfuls of well-rotted manure to the soil that you removed from the hole and mix the two.

4 If the plant has been well grown then you will not need to tease the roots out, but if the plant is at all pot-bound, spread some of them out. Now, still holding the plant with one hand on the top and one underneath, turn the plant over and carefully lower it into the hole.

5 Backfill around the plant with the manure/soil mixture. There is no need to put any of this mix under the plant as most "feeder" roots grow out laterally.

6 Firm the soil with your foot. If it is very wet, wait before you do this, as the firming may cause compaction and bad drainage. Water the plant generously to help the soil settle in around the plant and remove air pockets. Water at least once a week until established.

Topiary

The Japanese love clipping plants. Often this is simply to manage the growth of a tree or a shrub so that it doesn't become too overgrown, or it may be to allow more light into a garden or on to the mossy woodland floor. In many gardens in Japan, almost every shrub is clipped into rounded mounds, in layers or in squares. This clipping, known as *o-karikomi*, is something very familiar to Westerners when they think of Japanese gardens. But don't make the mistake of attributing very elaborate topiary to the Japanese, when that particular style is, in fact, more Chinese.

Above: *These massive blocks of clipped azaleas in Raikyu-ji resemble huge waves, cloud formations or even mountain ranges.*

AUTHENTIC STYLES

Topiary has been part of the way the Japanese have represented the abstraction of nature in their gardens since the earliest gardens of the Nara and Heian periods. It is worth taking a closer look at how the Japanese approach topiary. In the most famous traditional Japanese gardens, you will find very few examples of the kind of "cloud pruning" that you often find in copies of Japanese gardens, especially in the USA, where all kinds of plants from juniper to boxwood are clipped into a series of rounded "cloud" forms. These sculptured plants can be spectacular but can also, in the wrong setting, look rather comical. Topiary needs a skilled eye; without it, these plants can look more like clipped poodles than part of an elegant design. This brings us back to the recurring theme of the Japanese garden: that the overall composition should not be overwhelmed by excessive forms or colours that may be too distracting.

Although "cloud" pruning is an oriental practice, it was originally (and still is) highly developed in China and Korea. The practice of these countries influenced the art in Japan, but the Japanese way is different. The art of clipping shrubs, like so much of their art, is modest and meaningful when carried out by good designers. In the same way that the Japanese enjoy the simple and natural form of rocks while the Chinese enjoy eccentric and convoluted forms, Japanese garden designers also use their form of topiary with sensitivity and restraint. In the 16th and 17th centuries this practice of *o-karikomi* reached its peak of artistry. With consideration, it can be utilized in a Japanese garden in any of the main styles, using all kinds of plants.

Pines are often trained rather than clipped into remarkable shapes, but this is not strictly *o-karikomi*. These trees are restructured to imitate the weathered, windswept look of wild seaside and mountain-top pines – a favoured feature of many gardens.

Left: O-karikomi *reached its peak during the 17th century. Although the clipping in this garden imitates natural forms, the artistic hand is very apparent. The plants are made up of a mixture of azalea, camellia, pieris and photinia.*

Above: *This natural hill form of clipping has become popular In Western-style gardens. Sometimes all you have to do is follow the "desire" of the plant. Here, the result is a gentle flowing outline of a range of small hills.*

Below: *Planting azaleas or boxwood so that they can be clipped into rounded shapes of differing sizes will create a dynamic design, especially when placed to contrast with the natural outline of rocks.*

Above: *Cloud pruning is used to give plants an eccentric individual character. Although intriguing, these forms are not always easy to fit into an overall design, and are generally best placed as individual specimens.*

KOBORI ENSHU

The man acknowledged as the master of *o-karikomi* was Kobori Enshu (1579–1647). A soldier, town planner, tea-master and garden designer, Enshu introduced the clipping of great masses of evergreens, most often blocks of azaleas but using mixed plantings too, into abstract forms that suggested the movement of waves, the folding of hill ranges, and even, in the garden of Daichi-ji near Kyoto, a treasure-ship on an ocean. In the temple garden of Raikyu-ji, in Takahashi, Enshu combined the art of *o-karikomi* with the art of *shakkei*, clipping blocks of azaleas into forms that, in one part of the garden, imitate ocean waves around the Mystic Isles of the immortals, while in another the forms echo and draw in the outline of the surrounding hills. The overall effect makes for a brilliant composition.

AZALEAS IN TOPIARY

Clipping into such ambitious schemes is not the commonest form of topiary. It can also be the simple trimming of evergreen azaleas into rounded shapes on the banks of a small hill, by the side of a path or pond, or virtually anywhere in the garden. These shapes should complement each other. In the dry garden of Shoden-ji, the clipped azaleas are used in place of rocks and are arranged in artistic groups in a 3-5-7 arrangement, as in the Ryoan-ji. Rounded mounds of azaleas are often seen with square clipped hedges or camellias trimmed with a stem and a round head. This can be seen at Sanzen-in, in Ohara.

There are two varieties of azalea that are clipped differently. 'Hi-ra-do' is a large-leafed evergreen azalea, usually with pink or white flowers, that is clipped into large mounds, while 'Satsuki', with its tighter growth and deeper pink flowers, can be shorn very low, sometimes only 15cm (6in) from the ground. This technique can be used to make the azalea flow down hills, or hug the bases of rocks. Clipping, often carried out in spring and autumn, can result in many plump flower buds being removed.

Above: *This white-flowered form of* Camellia sasanqua *has been clipped into three layers. The autumn flowering should not be affected.*

Enough flower buds remain to give a display, but the number is moderate compared to the profuse flowering that azaleas might otherwise produce, often smothering the plant with so much colour that no leaf can be seen.

WHEN TO CLIP

To maintain a neatly trimmed look, follow these guidelines:

• azaleas, box, hollies and most other evergreens can be clipped from autumn to spring, preferably straight after flowering, followed later in the year by a gentle autumn tidy-up;

• hard prune in spring, to give the plant time to recover its vigour by the end of the growing season;

• avoid serious pruning from mid- to late summer, as this might stimulate a late flush of growth that is likely to be damaged by early autumn frosts.

Left: *This juniper,* Juniperus chinensis, *has been clipped into an elaborate Chinese-style "cloud" formation.*

SQUARE FORMS

Some gardens use linear hedge clipping to draw the eye into the garden or as a device across the line of vision to separate the foreground and background – a feature that actually unifies the composition more than it divides it. Rectangular topiary or clipping into square forms is more familiar in Western gardens. In Japan this kind of topiary and square shaping is used as an interplay between the architecture of the buildings and the informal landscapes beyond them. This may have been influenced by the culture of Western design, since this art developed in the 17th century when the Japanese were first exposed to Western culture after centuries of isolation.

By the 19th century (the late Edo period), much of the clipping of shrubs lost the genius of Enshu's art and became rather over-elaborate. This clichéd style has often been imitated by Western gardeners.

MIREI SHIGEMORI

In the 20th century, Mirei Shigemori (1896–1975), who was a landscape architect and scholar, transformed the design of the Japanese garden, incorporating old motifs and new together in a dramatically abstract manner. His work was also known for using the Western formality of squares, particularly in the gardens around the Hojo of Tofukuji. Here he used the device of repeated low squares of azaleas positioned in a chequerboard pattern.

PLANTS SUITABLE FOR *O-KARIKOMI*

Although deciduous shrubs could be used, the following plants are exclusively evergreen and are the most common ones used for *o-karikomi*:

Genus	Species	Common name
Rhododendron	various hybrid azaleas	azalea
Camellia	*sasanqua*	camellia
Camellia	*japonica* and others	camellia
Ilex	*crenata*	holly (Japanese holly)
Taxus	*baccata*	yew
Taxus	*cuspidata* and others	yew
Buxus	*sempervirens*	box
Buxus	*microphylla*	box

For large blocks and hedges of mixed evergreens, you could include:

Pieris	*japonica* and others	pieris
Photinia	*glabra* and others	photinia
Aucuba	*japonica* and others	spotted laurel
Prunus	*lusitanica*	Portugal laurel
Prunus	*laurocerasus*	cherry laurel
Nandina	*domestica*	heavenly bamboo
Osmanthus	*heterophyllus*	osmanthus
Osmanthus	*delavayi*	osmanthus
Osmanthus	*burkwoodii*	osmanthus
Taxus	*cuspidata*	yew
Taxus	*baccata*	yew
Thuja	*plicata*	western red cedar
Chamaecyparis	*obtusa*	hinoki cypress
Cryptomeria	*japonica*	Japanese cedar
Juniperus	*chinensis*	juniper

For clipping as individuals into cloud formations and other dramatic forms, choose:

Camellia	*sasanqua*	camellia
Osmanthus	*burkwoodii*	osmanthus
Prunus	*lusitanica*	Portugal laurel
Taxus	*baccata*	yew
Chamaecyparis	*obtusa*	hinoki cypress
Cryptomeria	*japonica*	Japanese cedar
Juniperus	*chinensis*	juniper

Far left: O-karikomi *can be used to enhance, or play with, existing architectural forms; this idea is similar in many ways to Western-style topiary.*

Left: *At Tofuku-ji, a Buddhist temple in Kyoto, Mirei Shigemori took some of the Western influence of topiary to create a chequerboard of clipped azaleas to evoke an old system of land use in China. The bold squares contrast with the white wall and its blackened vertical wooden posts.*

WATER FEATURES

The original Japanese word for landscape was *shan-shui*, meaning "mountain-water". Most Japanese gardeners find their inspiration in the mountain landscapes of their country, with their pools, tumbling streams and waterfalls. For this reason water and rocks have become central to Japanese garden design.

While sometimes it is the spirit of water that is encapsulated in dry water features such as waterfalls made with rocks, and streams and still areas of water constructed with sand or gravel, actual water features give lifeblood to any garden they are used in. This is true whether they are pond or stroll gardens with large ponds, meandering streams and natural waterfalls, or tea and courtyard gardens with smaller-scale examples of ponds and streams and self-contained features, such as *tsukubai* (water basins), *shishi-odoshi* (deer scarers) and *sui-kinkutsu* (echo chambers). At whatever level they are used, the Japanese are always meticulous about integrating water features sensitively within the garden landscape.

Above: *A waterfall in the gardens next to Himeji Castle, Japan.*
Left: *This pond view illustrates the technique of* shakkei, *a way of incorporating a distant view into a garden.*

Streams, waterfalls & ponds

Water has a naturally mesmerizing quality and it is easy to understand the spiritual significance of its various incarnations in the Japanese garden. The choice of Kyoto as the new capital in the 10th century was partly due to the way the hills frame the area, but also to the southward and westward flow of its rivers. In geomantic terms, the southward course towards the sun (fire) was said to bring life, growth and good fortune. While mountains were said to have a meditative quality, and were seen as symbols of the gods and the Buddha, water was a source of joy and detachment.

Above: *A naturalized stream in the Japanese garden at Newstead Abbey, England.*

WATER IN THE JAPANESE GARDEN

In the past, streams would have been used on ceremonial occasions in Japan as settings for poetry readings and for drinking tea and saki. They would typically lead in and out of shallow ponds, often home to koi and the common carp. Ponds were also combined with small islands, and a pine on an island is one of the classic images of Japan. The bridges that cross from the mainland to the island give a good viewing point for the fish and flowers in the shallow water.

Waterfalls are the third water element, believed by Japanese gardeners to be best placed where they can reflect the moon. This stunning effect can be recreated in your garden so long as you take care to place the waterfall so that it looks as natural as possible.

STREAMS

The first Japanese gardens of the Nara and early Heian periods had winding streams that bordered the courtyard before feeding the main pond. These were often edged with rocks, the two forming an important relationship. An august stone might be used to mark the headwater of the stream as it entered the garden. Other rocks would "follow the desire" of this stone, responding to its position and shape, forcing the water this way and that, changing its mood as it approached the pond. Mountainside, torrent-style streams required the scattering of many more random stones, which caused the stream to divide and flow rapidly through narrowing channels.

A *yarimizu* is a meandering stream of the type that might be found flowing through a meadow, and it can be used in gardens to create a wetland area including an estuary planted with reeds and irises – popular in the Japanese garden. The stream's point of entry into this wetland should be indiscernible, and the water level should be kept fairly high, like a flooded estuary. These estuaries are often crossed by zigzag, eight-plank bridges (*yatsuhashi*) that weave over iris beds or baskets of irises secured to the stream or pond bed. (See pages 144–145, *Making a yatsuhashi bridge*.)

Left: *This is a quintessential and perfectly enchanting Japanese garden at Hosen-in, Ohara. The pond reaches almost up to the veranda.*

STREAMS: KEY ELEMENTS

Assessing the flow A meandering stream will need a large pump to keep a good flow of water. The smaller the flow, the narrower the channel should be. Narrow channels will produce a more rapid flow.

Using intermittent flow If the flow is intermittent, make your stream into a series of small pools that have the look of a stream. This way, when there is no flow from a pump or a natural source, the stream bed will not empty out.

The sound of water Streams make a pleasant sound if allowed to trickle over stones and pebbles.

Planting Be careful not to let plants draw too much water from the sides of a stream. Thirsty plants can lower water levels considerably, so make sure the supply is always topped up.

Above: *With its naturally crushed quartzite beaches and well-formed boulders, the stream that tumbles down the mountains above Nagoya is shaded by groves of wild Japanese maples.*

Below: *Shigemori's double winding stream is highly abstract. The rocks, set in a naturalistic manner, contrast with the smooth-set cobbling and gravel beaches. The idea owes some of its inspiration to the streams of the Heian period.*

WATERFALLS

These are another essential feature of pond and stream gardens and stroll gardens. They are often built to represent the Buddhist Trinity, with one large stone at the centre, over which the water tumbles, supported on either side by two attendant stones that stand slightly further forward. Large and important waterfalls were often known as dragon-gate waterfalls after the Chinese symbol for waterfall, which included a dragon and water.

A stone might be placed at the waterfall's base to represent a carp, as if it were about to leap. This "carp stone" symbolized spiritual and mental effort in Buddhist and Confucian terms. The carp, symbolically, would change into a dragon on reaching the top of the waterfall. The carp stone points to the strivings of an individual to better themselves. It is also, on a more practical level, the part of the waterfall that receives the full force of the flow as it hits the bottom.

Above: *A thin stream of water falls on to a flat stone, creating a louder sound and making a more decorative pattern than if it had simply fallen into a pool of water.*

Left: *The eccentric rock forms in the Huntington Botanical Gardens are more Chinese in spirit, but the overall design follows the natural ethos of the Japanese.*

WATERFALLS: KEY ELEMENTS

Position Waterfalls will look too artificial if mounded up in the middle of a garden. Try to use a natural hill or slope near the edge of the garden.

Siting the inlet Try to disguise the inlet of the water as much as possible. To do this, choose a dark, mysterious corner of the garden for the emergence of your stream.

Installing a pump It will usually be necessary to use a circulating pump for artificial waterfalls.

Losing water It is easy to lose water down the sides of a waterfall through splashing, so be thorough and generous in laying out a liner beneath any nearby rocks and make sure the water is channelled back into the system.

PONDS

Whether it moves through a stream or waterfall, the water needs eventually to flow into a pond. In Japanese gardens, ponds tend to be no deeper than 45cm (18in), so that they are easily kept clean and clear, and the fish can be seen. Try to include a stream flowing out of the pond for authenticity, they are believed to carry away evil spirits. When planting the pond with lotuses (*Nelumbo*) or water lilies (*Nymphaea*), make sure that they do not become too choked or the pond may silt up after a few years.

The proposed design of the pond edges will determine what happens to

the water. For example, the water might appear to lap against a rocky shoreline, with a few solitary stones jutting out into the water, or it could become a wide inlet bordered by a sand bar. One sand-bar scene – the Aminoshidate peninsula in western Honshu – is so famous that it is cited as one of the three most important landscapes in Japan. It is often symbolically reproduced in Japanese gardens, often shown with a lantern on a promontory to represent a lighthouse. The shapes of ponds should, wherever possible, recall a natural scene, perhaps even the seaside.

The edges of ponds can be supported by rocks or timber posts. If you are using a pond liner, ensure that the liner is hidden by edging stones, timbers or plants. Japanese ponds are often designed using the shape of an ideogram, maybe symbolizing the word for "heart", "water" or "gourd", or they can be loosely outlined in the shape of a turtle or crane, however, it is more usual to find islands in these shapes representing the Mystic Isles.

ISLANDS

The islands in Japanese gardens might reproduce special scenes. The extraordinary rocky islets around Japan's main islands are very small,

but most have some kind of plant life, particularly pines, growing in their rocky crevices. The pine is a resilient tree that can take on fantastic forms as it is buffeted by salty winds. The Japanese take great care in pruning the pines in their gardens to give this characteristically wizened and windswept look.

Apart from the pine-covered island, there are other island styles, including the Rocky Islet and Cove Beach Island, all described in the *Sakuteiki*. The Meadow Isle is made up of low rocks, moss and autumn grasses. Forest Isles have random trees and grass, while Cloud and Mist Islands have sandy beaches planted in a spare, wispy way. These styles can all be recreated in your Japanese garden by growing suitable plants to set an atmospheric scene.

Islands were originally placed towards the middle of the pond, but slightly off-centre, to create a sense of mystery so that, whether you were boating or walking, you might find an inlet, waterfall, grotto, or even another island behind them. Use this element of surprise if you are designing a pond with islands.

Below: *In the gardens of Nijo Castle, the shogun used unusually large rocks as a means of exhibiting his own power.*

PONDS: KEY ELEMENTS

Shape Mimic the outline of natural ponds or choose a Japanese ideogram.

Using streams Most ponds have a wider inlet for the stream. This could be a good place to plant water irises.

Stepping stones When placing stepping stones across ponds with a butyl liner, make sure the liner is well protected from their weight.

Edging the pond Beware of how much the edges of a liner might show if there is a big drop in water level. Exposed liners are unattractive and can be damaged by animals and too much sunlight.

Position Choose a site where water might naturally lie in your garden.

Drainage Beware of any potential problems with drainage, and make provisions for overflow water.

Pumps Before buying a circulation pump for your pond, be aware of the running costs – it may have to run throughout the day to keep a pond healthy and clean.

Stocking a pond A pond with a good balance of plants and fish will stay naturally healthy.

Preparing the watercourse

Running water in the Japanese garden gives pleasure in terms of both sight and sound, but careful thought and planning is needed to make a water feature such as a stream or a series of cascades look natural. It may be easy to decide on the kind of feature you like, but its setting and the way it blends with other parts of the garden should be considered. As always, the preparation of the ground is vital, and you will need to use a variety of ground cover materials in the surrounding areas to hide tanks and pumps.

Above: *A carp stone at the base of a waterfall in the gardens of the Golden Pavilion. This tall upright stone is traditionally used in waterfalls.*

PREPARATION

Whether you are designing a broad, shallow stream to meander gently through the landscape (ideal for a flat site), or a rocky cascade feature (for a sloping garden), the watercourse first needs to be dug out as accurately as possible. Next you should remove any sharp stones. You will need a rubber liner, but before you lay this on the bed of the watercourse you should cover the channel with soft sand and/or a cushioning underlay to prevent the rubber liner being punctured. Specialist mail order companies and larger aquatic garden outlets will make a stream course liner for you, saving you the difficult task of manhandling, cutting and sealing a large, heavy piece of butyl rubber.

If you wish to make a waterfall on flat ground, the garden would have to be artificially contoured with the addition of several tonnes of soil, hardcore or subsoil covered with topsoil to achieve a suitable height. At the same time the rear of the waterfall feature should be camouflaged so that the water appears to be coming in from beyond the garden boundary. If this all sounds like a major upheaval, why not make a stream with a broader course on a gentle manmade slope instead? These can look and sound just as delightful in a Japanese garden.

ARRANGING THE ELEMENTS

Whether you are making your water feature on a natural or manmade gradient, carefully arrange the wall of rocks to create your cascade or waterfall, especially in the steeper sections. The strata and rock seams should line up to look as natural as possible. Use spare pieces of liner folded over several times to cushion the impact of large rocks sitting on the pool or stream liner and be careful not to tear the liner when arranging the stone.

Whatever liner you use, ensure that the overlapping pieces make a good seal and do not allow water to seep back through into the ground. For the same reason bring the edges of the liner well up on either side of the stream course, tucking them under the soil to hold them firmly in place to preserve the water.

Left: *This broad, meandering stream with gravel banks and large rocks in the Augsburg Japanese garden in Germany creates a restful scene. Artificial stream beds such as this are lined with butyl rubber.*

Camouflaging the water inlet and outlet of your stream requires a certain amount of ingenuity. For a re-circulating system where the stream appears to run through the garden, the water flows into an underground reservoir made by burying a plastic dustbin (trashcan), hidden by plants and perhaps a large slab of stone or a galvanized metal grill covered with pebbles and cobbles. Alternatively, the water can flow into a base pool or pond. A submersible pump sends water back from there to the top of the stream via a length of corrugated plastic delivery pipe buried underground and protected with a row of tiles.

Ask an aquatic or pond specialist to calculate the size of pump needed for your scheme and the diameter of delivery pipe required. You can do a rough estimation of the required flow rate by pouring measured buckets of water down the watercourse over a set time to achieve the look you want. Multiply up to calculate a litres-per-hour or gallons-per-hour figure.

A header pool, which could be made using a small, preformed fibreglass pond, at the top of a rock cascade ensures a steady flow of water with no sudden surges when the pump is switched on. The stream could also appear to rise directly from a spring, if you camouflage the end of the delivery pipe with rocks and plants.

Take time to select the piece of rock needed at the top of a large waterfall as it will be quite a feature even when the water is switched off. A flat spillstone on top ensures that the water curtain cascades evenly over the stone. Different shapes, sizes and arrangements of stones will affect the fall of water over cascades and, with careful positioning, a relatively small water output can be made to look like a much bigger flow. After cementing in the main rocks, experiment with loose stones, seeing how they can further deflect and direct the cascading water in a pleasing manner.

READY-MADE ALTERNATIVES

Stream courses and cascade features can be purchased ready made as rigid fibreglass sections, and are obtainable from aquatic specialist outlets as well as mail order or internet companies. These are fashioned to resemble rocky watercourses, but will need to be carefully camouflaged. This will be achieved by bedding them well into the earth and rock surroundings, giving them a more natural appearance. Adding gravel, pebbles and cobbles along the length of a fibreglass-lined or butyl rubber-lined stream softens the look, especially with the addition of overhanging plants and the occasional large rock or boulder.

Above: *Choose a preformed stream unit to blend in with the surrounding rocks and gravel.*

Above: *A preformed stream unit and water basin with a sandstone rock finish.*

Above: *Simple, dark stream liners may blend more easily. Use gravel to camouflage them.*

Building a meandering stream

Japanese gardens often have a meandering stream on a site where there is little natural gradient, and this is made using a flexible liner. The stream does not have to be dominated by rocks but can have softer, more rounded stones and boulders along its course, looking as if they have been deposited naturally along an old river bed. If you don't want to have a pump running continuously, the stream can be built as a very long narrow pool or series of pools with small falls along its length that are designed to overflow as soon as the pump introduces more water.

The header pool for a meandering stream does not have to be conspicuous – it simply provides the illusion of natural water entering the garden. The essential factor in creating a natural-looking scheme is to devise a wandering route that widens in parts and follows as closely as possible the direction that water would take naturally when flowing over a flat site.

The first thing to do is to check the garden levels. This is because even a relatively flat site will have a slope, no matter how slight. If you can identify the highest point, plan a scheme that has this as the source of the stream. This will not only avoid the difficulty of building the stream against a slope but also do away with the need to make slight changes in the levels.

Above: *This stream wanders through a moss-covered landscape. The shadowy enclosed garden and the shafts of sunlight breaking through give a feeling of solitude.*

Below: *The winding stream that runs into the large ponds at Motsu-ji has been restored to show how they were used during the 11th and 12th centuries. The placing of rocks and plants is understated, in the style of a slow stream weaving through a meadow.*

You will need

- string, canes or garden hose
- wooden pegs, about 2.5cm (1in) in diameter and 15cm (6in) long
- a hammer
- a straight-edged piece of wood
- a spirit level
- a spade
- a plastic sheet
- a rake
- underlay and flexible liner
- a thin, flat stone
- ready-mixed mortar
- a mortaring trowel
- cobbles or river gravel
- corrugated plastic pipe, measuring 1–2.5cm (⅜–1in) in diameter
- roof tiles
- rounded boulders
- a submersible pump
- a flow-adjusting valve

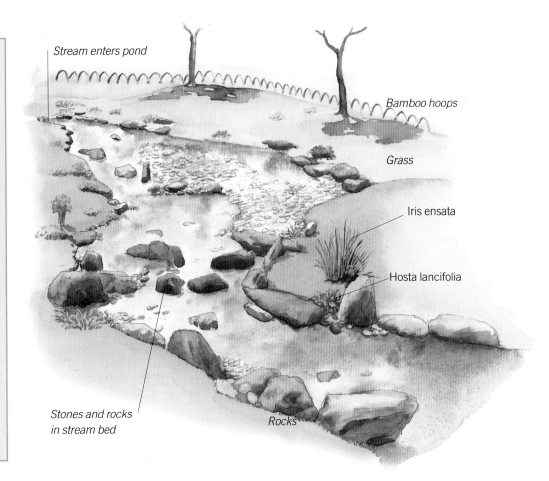

Stream enters pond

Bamboo hoops

Grass

Iris ensata

Hosta lancifolia

Stones and rocks in stream bed

Rocks

1 Having chosen the source, mark out the route of the stream with string, canes or a hose, working back from any existing pool.

2 Knock in the pegs about a metre (yard) apart along the route of the stream. Place a length of straight-edged wood and a spirit level on the pegs to identify any slight depressions or rises in the ground so that the surrounding soil can be adjusted if necessary. If the outlet point from the stream into the base pool is lower than the pool sides, there will be a flow when the pump is turned on. If this point is established first, then you can ensure that all the other edges are higher.

3 If the route of the stream is through a lawn, remove the turf and lay it elsewhere, if needed, or stack it upside down to rot down. Leave the pegs identifying the level in place.

4 Dig out the soil from the stream to a depth of 38cm (15in) in the centre. If the stream is wider than 60cm (24in), create shallow marginal shelves, 23cm (9in) deep, along the sides. Stack the soil on a *plastic* sheet to be used after the liner is inserted. Rake the stream bottom and the shelves to make them level, removing any sharp stones.

5 Place underlay along the stream length and drape the single length of liner into the stream contours. Use rocks to hold down the sides of the liner to stop them blowing about.

6 Create a spill point and prevent soil erosion by securing a thin, flat stone on the liner with a dab of mortar where the stream enters the pool.

7 Take some soil from the heap of topsoil and put it on the liner to form a shallow saucer shape inside the excavation. This will help to protect a cheap liner from ultra-violet light and provide a medium in which plants can grow. Top-dress the soil with rounded cobbles or river gravel to stop it from being washed away.

8 Bury a corrugated plastic delivery pipe along the side of the stream so that it runs from the base pool to the source. Cover the pipe with roof tiles before replacing the soil.

Above: *Winding streams are usually quite shallow, so care must be taken to disguise the liner at the edges, and cover the stream bed with varying sizes of gravels and cobbles.*

9 Position a few rounded boulders on the liner at the source to simulate a small spring.

10 Install a pump in the base pool and connect the outlet to the plastic delivery pipe. As the water will only trickle through this stream, a flow adjuster should be fitted to the delivery pipe to regulate the flow. Fill the pool with water and turn on the pump to check that the stream is running satisfactorily.

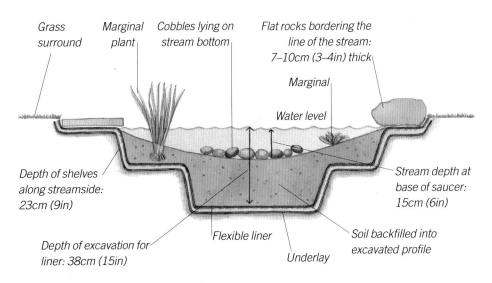

Grass surround

Marginal plant

Cobbles lying on stream bottom

Flat rocks bordering the line of the stream: 7–10cm (3–4in) thick

Marginal

Water level

Depth of shelves along streamside: 23cm (9in)

Stream depth at base of saucer: 15cm (6in)

Depth of excavation for liner: 38cm (15in)

Flexible liner

Underlay

Soil backfilled into excavated profile

Pond liners, pumps & filters

Pond liners and pumps are the invisible workers that enable you to create your Japanese water feature. They should never be seen, but are vital elements in the construction of a beautiful *tsukubai*, waterfall or stream. The pump ensures a constant supply of fresh, oxygenated water for fish, and special filtration systems help to keep water clear and process fish waste. The flow rate of a pump decreases over time so ensure you have spare capacity. Buy the best you can afford and you will be rewarded with a natural-looking water feature that lasts for years.

POND LINERS

Today's standard pond liner is made of black butyl rubber. It resists degradation by UV light and, being flexible, it is easy to fit and tolerant of stretching. It also resists puncturing and tearing. Undisturbed, good-quality butyl lining could last for thirty years. For naturalistic pools and ponds in Japanese gardens butyl is practical, versatile (fitting any irregular shape) and relatively easy to install compared to, say, a rigid fibreglass pond.

Butyl rubber comes in different grades, so discuss with your local aquatic garden specialist which will be suitable. For large ponds, liner made from one of the thicker grades could be very heavy and difficult to manoeuvre into position without several pairs of hands. The thickest grades are also less flexible and therefore trickier to lay or fold in tight bends and corners. Laying out the fabric on a sunny day allows it to warm up and become more flexible.

Above: *Wait a little while until the pond filters are mature before buying koi carp. Japanese koi are normally exported in November and December, but the best time to buy is in the spring when the water has warmed up.*

Below left: *The pool in this garden has been made with a flexible liner and is now being filled with water. The liner should not be exposed above the water line.*

Below: *This pool uses polythene (polyethylene) sheet as a flexible liner. Only trim the liner when you are certain the water level and edging are satisfactory.*

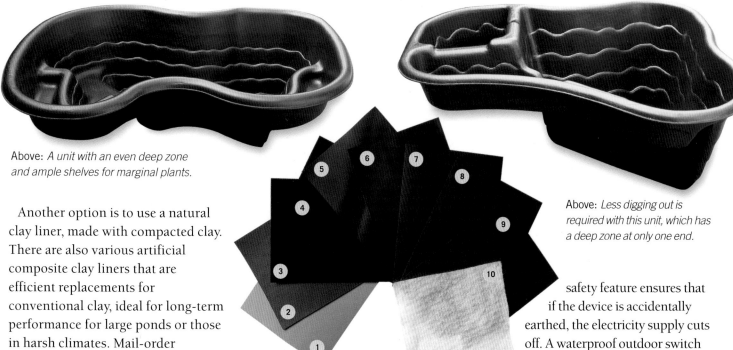

Above: *A unit with an even deep zone and ample shelves for marginal plants.*

Above: *Less digging out is required with this unit, which has a deep zone at only one end.*

Above: *Flexible liners are available in a variety of materials, thicknesses and colours. From left to right: 1 Butyl liner; 2 Butyl liner; 3 Low-density polythene (polyethylene); 5–9 PVC in different grades; 10 Underlay.*

Another option is to use a natural clay liner, made with compacted clay. There are also various artificial composite clay liners that are efficient replacements for conventional clay, ideal for long-term performance for large ponds or those in harsh climates. Mail-order companies specializing in pond liners or larger aquatic centres may offer a made-to-measure service.

Before you lay a flexible liner, you should use a geotextile membrane underlay to protect the butyl from being punctured by sharp stones and roots. You can use soft sand as an alternative, but the underlay is easier to keep in place over sharp corners and steep slopes. Use extra underlay and folded offcuts of butyl liner to provide a cushion beneath individual rocks and boulders laid on top of the liner. Always follow the manufacturer's instructions for the product that you buy.

Large schemes will require a submersible pump running off the mains (utility) voltage and so, unlike pumps operating via a transformer, the electrical cabling must be run through protective ducting buried to a depth of 60cm (24in). Make sure that you fit residual current devices (RCDs) or circuit breakers for all pieces of electrical equipment, including lighting. This safety feature ensures that if the device is accidentally earthed, the electricity supply cuts off. A waterproof outdoor switch can also be fitted.

FILTERS

For ponds containing fish, you will need a filtration system. This will either be a system submerged in the pond or, most efficiently, biological filters held in a header tank above the water. Fitting an ultra-violet clarifier causes green algae cells to clump together, making it easier for a biological filter to extract them. Fish and water lilies need a minimum pond depth of 45cm (18in) to overwinter, especially in colder regions. Consider installing a water heater for fish ponds, which keeps part of the surface ice-free.

PUMPS

For moving water features, such as streams or waterfalls, you will need a pump. Designs vary depending on the task they have to perform and they have different power outputs, so ask a water garden specialist to advise you. The data needed includes:
• the distance over which the water is travelling around the circuit
• the gradient
• the height of the starting point
• the diameter of the pipe
• the flow rate, which affects the appearance of a waterfall and speed of filtration.

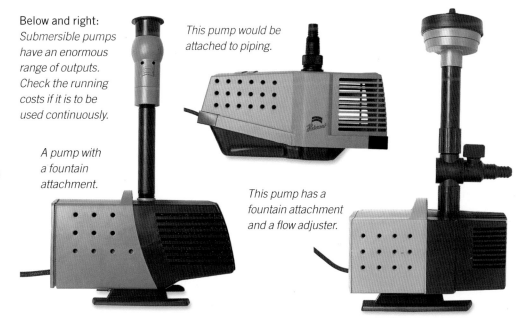

Below and right: *Submersible pumps have an enormous range of outputs. Check the running costs if it is to be used continuously.*

A pump with a fountain attachment.

This pump would be attached to piping.

This pump has a fountain attachment and a flow adjuster.

Creating edges for a pond

The edges of most small ponds, especially those in small gardens, are best lined with rocks. Larger ponds in stroll gardens, however, often include stretches of cobbled beaches or grass rolling up to the very edge of the pond. The edges of ponds always need careful attention, as the water may run out or evaporate and this leaves an ugly view of the liner. Whichever kind of edging you choose, make sure that it covers the edge of the pond well and that it is a practical solution for the kind of pond you have made.

CONCEALING A POND LINER

If you are using a butyl liner, make sure that you conceal 10cm/4in of the liner below the water line with rocks or gravel, and any part of the liner that might show above water level. Bear in mind that in summer, with increased evaporation, the pond level may drop and expose the liner. It is also worth noting that butyl liners deteriorate more quickly when exposed to sunlight and frost.

ROCK EDGING

The rocks around a pool should be partially submerged to achieve a natural effect. The rocks will also need to be supported on a foundation slab or concrete footing.
• If you are using a liner, pass it over the slab or footing and under the rock, embedding the liner into a layer of stiff mortar or concrete.
• You can use a sandwich of underlay above and below the liner to help protect it.
• Ensure that the liner finishes above the level of the water under the rock at the side of the pool.

COBBLE EDGING

The essential thing in introducing naturalness to a cobble edge is to arrange the sizes so that the main body of cobbles increases in diameter from below the waterline into the drier margins.

• Sort your cobbles into size before you lay them.
• To prevent the cobbles from rolling to the pool bottom, a concrete support should be constructed at the edge.

GRASS EDGING

An edging of grass is very easy on the eye and is suitable for larger pools and stroll gardens.
• The edge of the pool can become worn fairly quickly, which can cause the sides to crumble.
• Avoid this by underpinning the turf with a small foundation of stones or timber edging (see below right).

Above: *Cobbled beaches are popular around ponds, at times set loosely and at others set in mortar to create an even surface.*

TIMBER EDGING

An alternative method of taking grass up to the water's edge is to construct a vertical timber wall, which will extend from below the waterline to just below the level of the grass. The timber wall looks most attractive if it is made with timber rounds, at a measurement of 5–7.5cm (2–3in) in diameter. These are placed tightly side by side to form a palisade-like barrier. Proprietary lengths of "log roll" could also be used

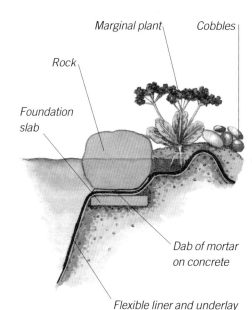

Rock edging *A rock that is being used at the edge of a pool is best when it is partially submerged, and supported with a foundation slab under the liner.*

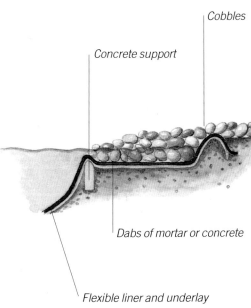

Cobble edging *To prevent cobbles from rolling into the deeper zone of the pond, make a shallow shelf with a raised edge under the flexible liner in order to give extra stability.*

instead of complete rounds, and these log rolls are already joined together by galvanized wire strands.

• To make either of these systems of timber edging stable enough not to crumble into the pool, a small trench, approximately 15cm (6in) deep and 10–15cm (4–6in) wide, must be dug out at the pool edge.

• A concrete support should be added in front of this trench.

• The pool liner is then run over the concrete support and into the trench, finishing above the waterline.

• A mix of stiff mortar is placed on the liner and the timbers bedded into the stiff mortar before it hardens. Make sure that the timber rounds are straight and tight together because they cannot be moved once the mortar sets.

• After a day or two, when the mortar has set hard, soil can be backfilled behind the timber edge and the liner can be wedged upright so it is held above the waterline.

• Turf can then be laid right up to the timber edge on the fresh soil, which is now supported by the concrete at the water's edge.

PAVED EDGING

A more formal and solid design can be made with paving stones arranged around the edge of the pond.

• Prepare the area by scraping away some topsoil. If the subsoil is not firm, replace it with 7.5–10cm (3–4in) of hardcore. Top this with about 5cm (2in) of damp sand, rake and level, then cover with the underlay and liner.

• Place the perimeter paving stones along the water's edge, checking that they fit well and that they overlap the water by 2.5–5cm (1–2in). Use the largest piece to give stability, with the straight edge overlapping the water.

• Mix some mortar on a board, then lay the first stones on to dabs of mortar trowelled on to the liner.

• Press the slab down on to the mortar dabs and bed it down firmly before laying the adjacent slabs.

• Check the slabs are level with a spirit level. To adjust the height, tap with a club hammer over a block of wood.

• The gaps between the slabs must be filled with a fairly wet mortar mix in order to hold each slab in place. Lay on a slight slope to reduce run-off from any adjacent paving or grass.

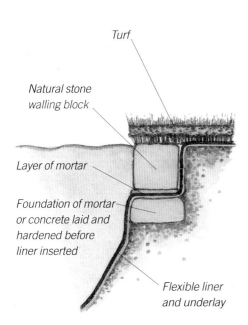

Grass edging *A grass edge is subject to heavy wear and tear. It should be supported by a natural stone walling block, which is placed on a deep foundation of stiff mortar or concrete.*

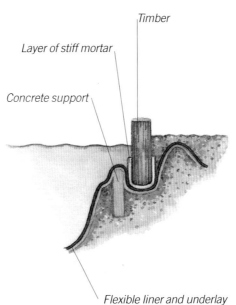

Timber edging *Log roll or timber rounds placed side by side make a good edge when mortared into a thin trench under the level of the water. Turf edging can then be run up to the timber edging.*

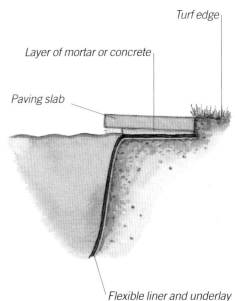

Paved edging *When using a paving slab to provide an edge, ensure that there is a small overlap above the water, and mortar the slab on to the liner above a foundation of hardcore.*

Tsukubai & shishi-odoshi

Some Japanese gardens contain very distinctive water features called *tsukubai,* or water basins. These water basins were often found in traditional tea gardens and were used for providing drinking water. They were usually fed by a natural spring. Taller basins, *chozubachi,* are sited nearer the house. Another traditional Japanese water feature, the *shishi-odoshi,* was designed as a deer scarer and uses running water to make a knocking noise with a bamboo pole against a stone basin, a sound loud enough to deter marauding animals from eating tender plants in the garden.

Above: *Water basins were traditionally made from stone and were fed with water from a bamboo spout called* kakei.

WATER BASINS

The principle of spiritual and physical cleanliness has been adapted for use in Japanese garden design from the earliest days. You will often find a water basin or other standing water feature in a Japanese garden, and sometimes even two or three such features.

Water basins are not always kept full, except those that are fed from a concealed bamboo pipe that is allowed to drip into the basin to keep the water fresh, rippling and constantly overflowing. Water basins that are not automatically filled will need cleaning out and topping up with fresh water. In addition, just as the path can be cleaned and damped down before the guests arrive, the sides of stone water basins may also be wetted to darken and intensify the natural colours and markings of the stone.

The water basin itself may be a simple rounded bowl carved from a single piece of granite, but traditional designs (copied from various historic shrines and temples in Japan) vary, and some are surprisingly geometric, cube-shaped or cylindrical, with carved patterns and designs around the outside. These intricate designs tend to stand out more than the rustic bowls, making a pleasing contrast to the surrounding rock forms and

Above: *A 17th-century crouching basin in the temple garden of the Ryoan-ji. This has been one of the most copied of all water basins.*

Above: *A cube-shaped water basin with regular square indentations in a private garden in Ohara. This design, made from granite which has* tarnished and discoloured over time, is copied from an original basin in the gardens of the Silver Pavilion, or the Ginkaku-ji Temple in Kyoto, Japan.

plantings. Nowadays, materials other than granite are often used, and the more porous they are, the more quickly they will develop a pleasing patina of age due to the moist environment.

There should be good drainage around a basin, as the fact that the basin is frequently topped up, and so overflows, could make the area swampy. If the basin is being refilled constantly from a pipe, a drain will also be needed to take the water away. The area around the water basin is often surrounded by cobbles or large-sized gravel to keep it dry. This combination of gravel and water basin is another opportunity to express artistry. You can place a special stone that does not get wet in the surrounding gravel area for people to stand on.

TALL WATER BASINS

Although tall water basins come in all shapes, sizes and materials, such as cut and natural stone, ceramic and wood, there are essentially two types: *chozubachi* and *furisode*.

Chozubachi basins are usually up to 1m (3ft) high and are placed on verandas where they can easily be reached from the house. These basins may have a slatted bamboo cover to keep the water fresh, to stop birds from drinking there and to prevent leaves and debris from falling in.

Furisode basins come in the form of a narrow, naturally rippled rock that is shaped like the long sleeve of a kimono. A bowl is carved into the stone, sometimes in the shape of a gourd. (The gourd is a symbol of good hospitality, being the traditional holder for the Japanese rice wine sake.)

A more elaborate tall basin can be found in some Japanese gardens, one example being the *ginkakuji*, which is named after the famous garden of the Silver Pavilion, near Kyoto, with tiled patterning on the sides.

LOW, OR CROUCHING, WATER BASINS

The *tsukubai chozubachi* is a low, or crouching, basin placed on or just off the *roji* (the path to the tea house). The act of crouching to reach the basin, like the bending needed for the middle crawl-through gate and the tea house's small hatch-like entrance, compels guests to humble themselves.

One famous anecdote recalls how the great tea master Rikyu had hidden the view of the beautiful inland sea in his tea garden with dense plantings. His guests and visitors could see the view only at the moment when they bowed down to cleanse themselves at the *tsukubai*. This is a perfect expression of Zen – that true beauty is available to us only once we have lowered our heads (and therefore our minds) lower than our hearts.

CHOOSING A WATER BASIN

Water basins were originally made of granite, which makes them very heavy and therefore expensive to transport. However, fake stone (fibreglass), glazed ceramic and concrete versions are easy to come by nowadays and may be found in garden centres, especially those that specialize in Japanese garden ornaments.

Above: *A simple* tsukubai *will work in naturalistic settings as well as in Zen gardens.*

Above: *Still quite simple, this flower-like* tsukubai *looks best in plain surroundings.*

Above: *This* tsukubai *is hewn out of a rock, a dramatic feature with a strong presence.*

Above: *This reproduction, like many others, is based on original Japanese designs.*

Above: *This cube-shaped* tsukubai *would make a good courtyard feature.*

Left: *Purification is ritualized by the Japanese. Outside all Buddhist and Shinto shrines there are water basins for cleaning the hands and mouth.*

Below left: *Two tall water basins (*chozubachi*) that can be reached from the veranda of Sanzen-in, in Ohara. These are square basins set on stone pillars.*

disapproved of an approach that meant everything was too rigidly correct. For instance, it is traditional to place the *tsukubai* on the sunny side of the path, so that guests do not have the sun on their backs and necks when they kneel down to take water from it. This kind of tradition is just respectful, intended to be attentive to the comfort of the guest, and it is therefore not necessary to copy it precisely. The key consideration here is that the exact placement depends on the conditions within the garden – if it is shady enough, your guests will not need to shelter from the sun.

There are often special stone arrangements around the basin, featuring worn, rounded cobbles and pebbles, with accompanying stones, a lantern, ferns and evergreen shrubs. Often a special flat-topped stone is placed to the side of the basin for guests to stand on or to rest their fan or bag.

In wooded wilderness settings, the arrangement can be quite lush and atmospheric, but as with so much that is connected with the tea ceremony, the *tsukubai* is full of symbolism. This gives the garden designer plenty of opportunities to take the concept of the *tsukubai* and the lantern that often accompanies it, to abstract it and give it a modern interpretation, as befits a contemporary garden.

The fact that water basins symbolize cleanliness and hospitality means that they are not only found in tea gardens or off the verandas of houses: they will also be found in courtyard gardens and along passageways to the house.

As well as this, pottery or stone urns can be used, and these make excellent alternatives.

Recycled materials are another option – maybe some hollow, second-hand architectural pillars, or old *stupas* (a feature in many Buddhist temples). So use anything that might take on a new life as a water basin, including old stone water troughs or a stone with a natural deep depression.

PLACING A WATER BASIN

A *tsukubai* should always be placed by a path and a *chozubachi* by a house, but apart from that there is no need to get too caught up in the idea that everything should be set exactly according to a pre-ordained plan. Japanese gardeners do not consider this to be in the true spirit of Zen. In fact, Rikyu, the master of the Japanese tea ceremony, would have

Below *A stone basin, or* tsukubai, *covered with moss in the gardens at Ten Juan Temple, Kyoto.*

Below: *Water basins are often filled constantly by fresh water, the excess draining away among rocks and pebbles. A sump could be built under the stones to collect the water, which can then be recycled using a submersible pump.*

Above *Visitors to the Meiji Shrine in Tokyo, Japan, use the traditional bamboo ladles provided for washing and purification.*

Below *This basin in the Seiryu tea garden at Nijo Castle is carved from natural rock.*

Above: *The water in a* shishi-odoshi *is circulated with a small pond pump, placed below water level in a bowl, and hidden with a metal grill and stones. One outlet makes the water surface ripple and the other trickles into the swinging arm.*

DEER SCARERS (*SHISHI-ODOSHI*)

Another traditional Japanese garden water feature, the *shishi-odoshi*, or deer scarer, is sometimes found in kit form in garden centres, but you are likely to find more authentic-looking *shishi-odoshi*, or the individual elements and raw materials for making your own, from specialist Japanese garden suppliers. This can be an enjoyable do-it-yourself project, and means you can choose the elements to fit with your garden.

The *shishi-odoshi* consists of a piece of bamboo 60–90cm (24–36in) long, drilled through to accommodate a pin on which it pivots. One end rests on a piece of stone called a sounding rock and the other end fills with water fed from a bamboo spout. When it contains enough water, the pivoting bamboo tips, releasing the water, and then flips back up, striking the stone and making a noise. This is very similar in basic construction to the *tsukubai*, with an underground, camouflaged reservoir containing a submersible pump and a length of plastic tubing that links the pump to the bamboo feed pipe.

Above: *This deer scarer was featured in Horoshi Namori's show garden at the Chelsea Flower Show, London, in 1996.*

Below: *A traditional Japanese fountain, the* shishi-odoshi *was originally used to deter deer from feeding on shoots in rice paddies.*

Making a *sui-kinkutsu*

A *sui-kinkutsu* is a water echo-chamber, or more literally a "water harp chamber". It is constructed so that you can listen to the dripping of water falling into an underground chamber by means of a hollow bamboo pipe held to the ear at one end and to a hole in the ground above the chamber at the other. The sound is like that of the traditional stringed Japanese musical instrument called the *koto*. This might also make you think of a stream in a mountain cave. In very quiet surroundings you should be able to hear the sound without the aid of a bamboo pipe.

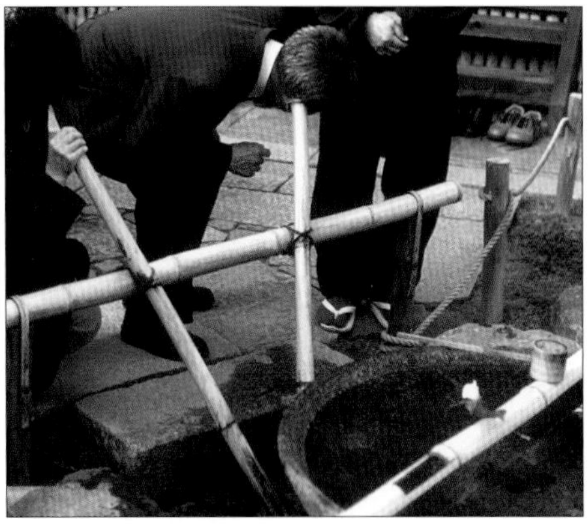

Above: *The idea behind the* sui-kinkutsu *is to create "music" from the sound of water, like a waterfall dripping in a mountain cave.*

Purists believe that a *sui-kinkutsu* should be constructed only in conjunction with a *tsukubai* arrangement (see pages 116–120), as it collects water dripping and draining away from the water basin, which is itself fed by a dripping bamboo pipe. However, a *sui-kinkutsu* may also be constructed as a separate feature, independently from a *tsukubai*, perhaps simply collecting water from a dripping hose that is switched on especially for visitors or at your personal discretion.

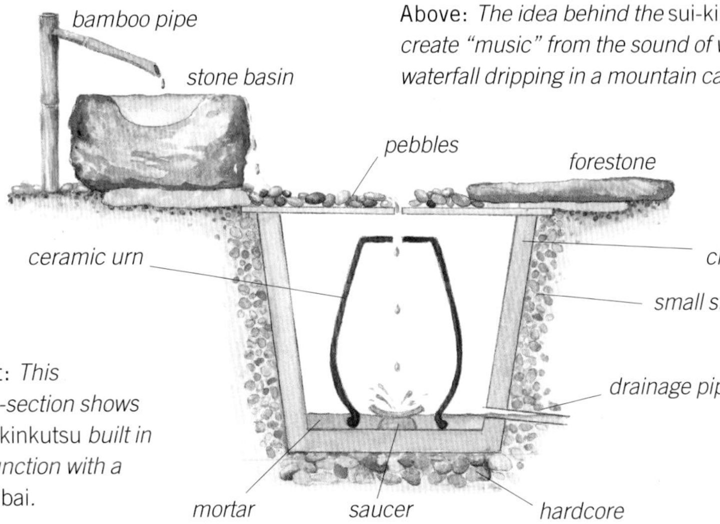

bamboo pipe
stone basin
pebbles
forestone
ceramic urn
chamber
small stones
drainage pipe
mortar
saucer
hardcore

Right: *This cross-section shows a* sui-kinkutsu *built in conjunction with a* tsukubai.

You will need

- a piece of cylindrical shuttering or an old plastic barrel
- concrete mix, 1 part sand to 4 parts cement
- an Ali-Baba-style urn about 80–100cm (32–40in) high and 40cm (16in) in diameter with a single drainage hole in thits base
- a small ceramic plant saucer
- rope to lower the pot
- a paving slab, 1m (40in) square, with a hole 4cm (1½in) wide drilled in the centre

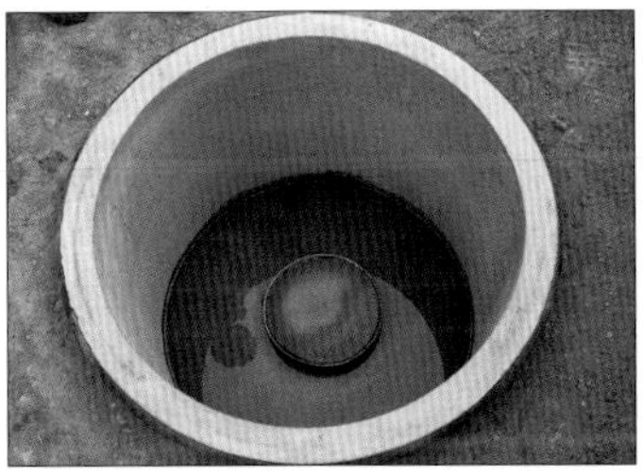

1 Dig out a pit around 1.2m (4ft) deep and 1m (40in) wide. Create a circular shuttering around 70cm (28in) in diameter using an old plastic drum or some other mould that can be removed easily after surrounding it in concrete. Line the base of the hole and the outside of the mould with 8–10cm (3–4in) of concrete. Make sure the bottom of the hole is level. Make a drainage outlet 10cm (4in) above the bottom of the chamber to take the excess water away to a soakaway or an approved watercourse.

2 Leave the concrete to set for two days before removing the mould and proceeding with the next stage.

3 Place the ceramic saucer at the bottom of the hole. The saucer should be smaller than the rim of the vase.

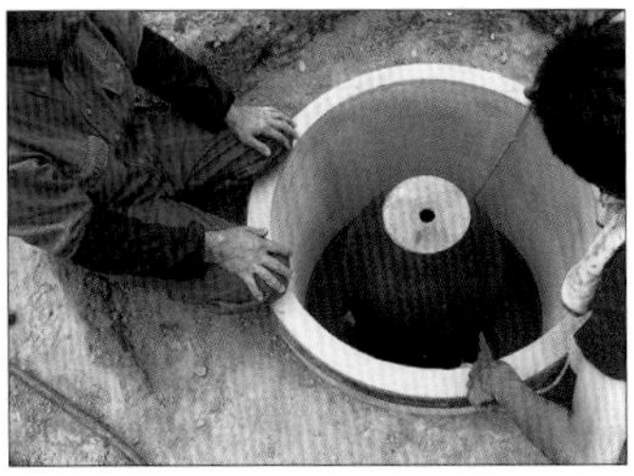

4 Tie a rope around the rim of the Ali Baba vase and (with assistance to balance the weight) lower the upturned vase carefully into the chamber so that it completely covers the saucer, with the drainage hole directly above it.

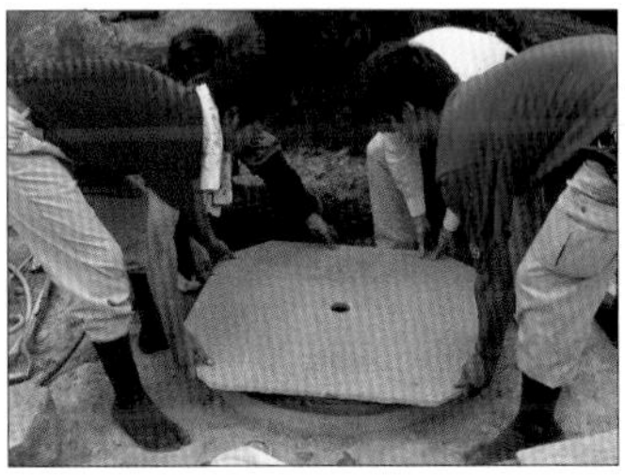

5 Lay the paving slab over the chamber. Then direct your chosen water source to the hole in the paving slab.

6 You will need to disguise the paving slab and the water source (for example a hose). You can do this using small stones and cobbles. An alternative camouflage idea is to place a water basin over the slab, but position it off-centre so that the water spilling out of the basin finds its way into the hole above the chamber.

Constructing a reservoir

Water basins and deer scarers both need a reservoir and pump to make a circulating water system, unless they have a natural source of water. The reservoir for the water will sit immediately under the water basin (which is usually made from a hollowed-out rock, but any basin that is dignified enough, including a stone trough, could be used) or at the spilling end of the deer scarer, and it gives the illusion that the water feature is stream fed. If the site is in a windy location, check that all the water flows back into the reservoir, otherwise it can empty, causing the pump to burn out.

The amount of water that circulates around a water basin is much the same as that for a deer scarer (*shishi-odoshi*), where both require a mere trickle for best effect. Thus the reservoir need be no more than 100 litres (22 gallons). The reservoir can be set almost directly below the feature, but in a place where you can access it for cleaning, and where, if it were to overflow, there is some suitable drainage around it.

The small amount of water spillage likely from the basin will not need an extensive drainage system, but it is a good idea to cover the immediate area around the reservoir with loose stones and gravel to aid drainage. This will also give a more authentic appearance.

Above: *Ladles are laid over or by the side of the basin supported by a rack of bamboo. Guests use them to cleanse their hands, mouths and faces before entering the tea house.*

Below: *The* shishi-odoshi *reservoir differs little from that of a water basin. Always ensure that the spillage goes back into the reservoir.*

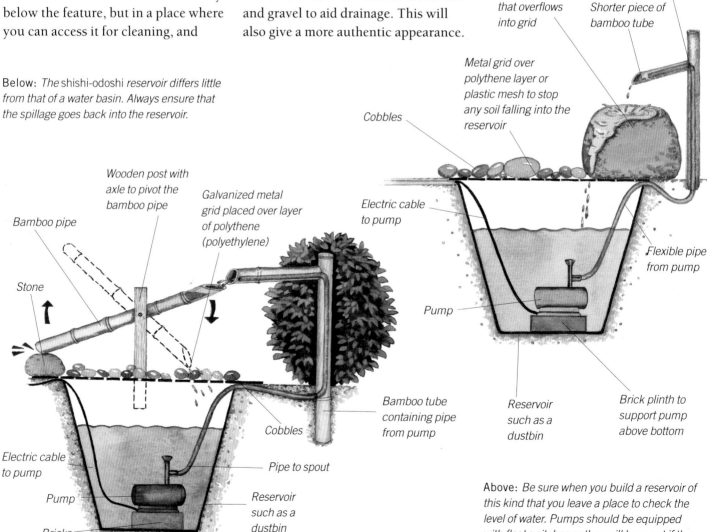

Hollowed-out stone basin that overflows into grid

Pipe inside bamboo tube

Shorter piece of bamboo tube

Metal grid over polythene layer or plastic mesh to stop any soil falling into the reservoir

Cobbles

Electric cable to pump

Flexible pipe from pump

Pump

Reservoir such as a dustbin

Brick plinth to support pump above bottom

Wooden post with axle to pivot the bamboo pipe

Bamboo pipe

Galvanized metal grid placed over layer of polythene (polyethylene)

Stone

Electric cable to pump

Pump

Bricks

Cobbles

Pipe to spout

Bamboo tube containing pipe from pump

Reservoir such as a dustbin (trash can)

Above: *Be sure when you build a reservoir of this kind that you leave a place to check the level of water. Pumps should be equipped with float switches or they will burn out if the reservoir is allowed to dry out.*

You will need

- a reservoir kit from a specialist supplier, which should include a reservoir, a metal grid, a sheet of plastic mesh, a polythene layer, a small pump with a cable, and a length of ribbed hose to join the pump to the delivery pipe of the deer scarer or water basin

Or you can make your own kit using

- a strong plastic bin at least 60cm (24in) deep and 45cm (18in) wide, such as a cold-water storage tank sold for central heating systems
- a small pump kit from your local aquatic centre – the pump should have a variable pressure valve so that you can modulate the flow
- a polythene layer to cover the bin
- a sheet of plastic mesh
- a metal grid, which can be made of a piece of concrete reinforcing mesh from a builder's merchant

For both options, you will also need

- lengths of pre-drilled bamboo tubes to deliver water to the feature
- some cobbles or large gravel
- a spade to dig a hole
- some sharp sand
- a spirit level
- a waterproofed electrical source or socket for the pump

1 Choose a small, level site. The cobbles can extend as far as you wish, but the area need be no bigger than a circle of the diameter of the reservoir. Mark out the diameter and dig out a hole wider and deeper. Line the base and sides with sharp sand to protect the reservoir from stones and to make it level.

3 Backfill the gap between the reservoir and the hole sides with soil and ram it until firm with a piece of timber, such as a cut-down broom handle. Rake the surrounding soil and remove any stones.

5 Before lowering the submersible pump on to the plinth, attach a flexible delivery pipe to the pump outlet. Take the pipe over the side of the reservoir (or through a hole in the top edge) and push it through a tube of bamboo, 60–90cm (2–3ft) tall, next to the reservoir.

2 After placing a 4–6cm (1½–2½in) deep layer of sand at the bottom of the hole, lower the reservoir into the hole and check that the rim is just below the edge. Then check that the sides are level with a spirit level. If necessary, you will need to adjust the base of the hole until it is completely flat.

4 Remove any soil from inside the reservoir as, if it is left, this may silt up the pump and stop it functioning. Make a plinth in the reservoir with two bricks or a piece of broken paving.

6 Push the pipe through to a further bamboo spout positioned to spill into the basin. These can be made by cutting away the end of the pipe. Lay the polythene layer over the depression and the reservoir and cut out a hole 5cm (2in) smaller than the bin diameter.

7 Lay the galvanized metal grid on top of the reservoir. This should be larger than the diameter of the top of the reservoir. Fill the reservoir with water.

8 Lay a sheet of plastic mesh over the grid to stop any soil falling into the reservoir. Position the spill basin at the side of the grid, but make sure that it slightly overhangs the reservoir so that it will overflow on to the cobbles.

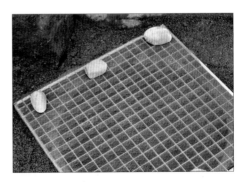

9 Test the flow of water, adjusting the regulator on the pump or moving the position of the spout so that the water falls into the saucer part of the spill basin. Arrange the cobbles over and around the metal grid. Test the system to make sure there is minimal water loss through spillage or splashing, and adjust accordingly.

CREATIVE CONSTRUCTS

This chapter looks at the elements that are designed and created to fit within the Japanese garden. Manmade constructs such as paths, fences, bridges, lanterns and water basins add form, character and scale to a garden. When used well, these can contribute to its beauty. Such artefacts are not placed to be admired as sculpture as in Western gardens, but blended into their surroundings to form an intrinsic part of the whole composition.

The Japanese garden designer is deeply interested in the quality of these objects, choosing them very carefully so that they form part of the design of the garden. Most fences and garden buildings are built of raw timber, bamboo, sisal and reeds, exhibiting the pure natural qualities of those materials, while lanterns and water basins are often carved out of the finest stone and encouraged to weather. Paths and bridges should be designed with great care and creativity, using a combination of natural materials and balancing the gardener's deliberate artistry with nature's own perfection.

Above: *A path in a bamboo grove near the Tenryu-ji Temple.*
Left: *A Japanese garden, featuring a curved bridge, ablaze with the colours of autumn.*

Paths

Japanese garden paths have evolved from the simple surfaces of gravel and fine sand that were originally used for paths that circled around ponds, to the stepping-stone paths of the tea garden where each step carries a special significance for the traveller. Some of the path styles used today are simple and naturalistic whereas others use a highly sophisticated mix of materials and designs. The only requirement is that whichever kind of path you choose, it should blend well with the natural style of your garden.

Above: *Ginkgo leaves fall on to a path. Paths are often edged in imaginative ways.*

THE PURPOSE OF PATHS

The main purpose of paths is to control the visual experience of the stroller, with each change of direction introducing a new view. From the earliest times, paths were designed to stop or turn abruptly – a device that encourages the stroller to hesitate and scan a view that was deliberately composed to be seen from a particular spot. Zigzag paths and bridges take this idea to a greater extreme.

Paths found their true significance in the tea garden and were originally known as dewy paths (*roji*). The tea path recalls the pilgrimages that philosophers, painters and Zen monks made on their visits to China in search of renowned Chinese artists and sages, who lived, often alone, in huts and hermitages in the hills and mountains. As the tea guest is drawn along the *roji*, they are made more conscious of each step they take through the use of stepping stones. These had previously been used only for practical purposes: to cross water and swampy, muddy ground. Their addition to the tea garden was initiated by Rikyu, who was one of the great Japanese tea masters of the 16th century.

The strategic placement of some larger stepping stones on a path gives the visitor the freedom to be less conscious of where their feet are falling. This means that they would be able to look up to take in a special view of the garden or cleanse themselves at a water basin. Stepping stones were always kept scrupulously

Left: *The formality of this path cutting through the dry garden of Tenju-an is softened by an enveloping carpet of moss. The path takes a sudden right-angled turn at the end, a black pine (Pinus thunbergii) grows alongside it.*

Above: *In some climates, moss will readily creep over gravel paths, and may create a desirable effect.*

Above right: *In the gardens of Rheinaue in Bonn, Germany, a naturalistic path of stepping stones set in gravel crosses a cobbled path, which gives way to more formalized paving set in grass.*

clean, brushed and even damped down to give the impression of mountain dew. Damping down paths is considered to be a very hospitable way to welcome guests into a tea garden or the tea house itself. However, great care must be taken to keep stepping stones free of slimy algae, which can become extremely slippery when wet.

In some Japanese gardens, especially dry ones – which were mostly designed to be viewed from one particular place, such as the veranda of a building – the paths of stepping stones might be set to weave right across the garden. In the past, these paths were rarely walked on, but were used by the garden designers of the day to suggest movement and to draw the viewer's eye across a particular scene. If a path was not

EDGING GRAVEL PATHS

Gravel is a loose material, so it is always best to contain it carefully within solid edges. If you don't edge these paths, the gravel will tend to get pressed into the surrounding soil or kicked around and will eventually disappear.

Edging materials	Where and when to use
Paving and cobbles	Paving stones or cobbles should be chosen for the appropriateness of their setting. Make sure the size and shape of paving stones complements the surrounding garden.
Granite setts	Near the house, more formal granite setts might be used.
Random stones and other materials	In more naturalistic areas you could choose to use random stones. In Japanese gardens it is common to find imaginative use of all kinds of "found" materials such as old roofing tiles, long strips of chiselled granite or even charred post tops. Such elements need to be placed with great sensitivity.
Wood and steel	The use of easy-to-install wooden boards and steel edging would be possible in any area, as these materials are subtle and will blend in with the surrounding shrubs or mossy areas, especially once they have weathered. Steel is best used sparingly for a more authentic design.
Bent bamboo	Paths in Japanese parks and some private gardens are edged in hoops of bent bamboo, which adds style and rhythm to the path, as well as discouraging visitors from stepping on the garden.

Right: *Changes in path angles encourage the stroller to take in new views. The random paving stones in this path at Koto-in are bordered by long rectangular strips of granite.*

supposed to be taken, for reasons of privacy or in order to delay the tea guests from entering the inner tea garden, a small, round boulder bound with a knotted string, rather like a small parcel, would be left in the middle of a paving stone. This would indicate to any visitors to the garden that the path was not yet meant to be used for crossing the space.

SAND AND GRAVEL

By the Kamakura period (1185–1392), when the first stroll gardens were constructed, garden paths were likely to have been laid with a mixture of compacted fine sand and a light grit surface, similar to the one used for ceremonies in the courtyards of Heian residences. Both materials are readily available today. Although gravel paths need maintenance, they are one of the easiest and cheapest means of providing an all-weather surface in gardens, particularly in rainy climates such as that of Japan. The paths need to be topped up occasionally with fresh gravel, weeded and then raked or brushed with bamboo brooms.

PAVING AND COBBLING

Whole paths are frequently made with randomly or formally arranged paving or cobbling. There are numerous designs to choose from, as shown on pages 130–131. The joints between the paving or cobbling are usually filled with compacted sharp sand, which is a good medium for the colonization of moss. If the moss is left uncontrolled in damp climates, it may grow until it almost envelops the surface; this is not always discouraged, because moss is both natural and beautiful.

In many Japanese gardens, the paths do become soft and mossy and this is a perfect surface to wander on. You can fill the joints of paved areas with a soft cement mix (1 part cement to 12 parts sand) to give a firm binding but also grow less vigorous mosses and other plants. To exclude all vegetation between the joints, use a stronger mix (1 part cement to 6 parts sand).

DRAINAGE

Even on loose gravel paths, make allowance for the run-off of surface water. This is best done by creating a slight camber to the path, by sloping one side or raising the middle so that excess water can run off to one or both sides. This will be important on sloping paths, where heavy rain can cause erosion. On solid paved areas, provision may need to be made with land drains and soakaways, especially on poorly drained ground.

WIDTH OF PATHS

You can make gravel paths as little as 1m (1yd) in width, but bear in mind that only one person will be able to walk down the path at one time. If paths are too narrow, rain-soaked shrubs will wet you as you pass. If you want to be able to walk two abreast, the minimum path width should be 1.5m (5ft), though a more comfortable width for two people would be 2m (7ft), which will allow for plants that have grown over the sides of the paths.

Tea paths that are made of stepping stones are designed for one person to pass along them at a time. The width of such a path will depend on the design effect and how comfortable you want the path to feel. Some tea paths in Japan can be quite tricky to negotiate. This is a deliberate device, used to make the guest much more aware of each step they take. If you want to achieve a more relaxed stroll, then place the stones about 70–80cm (28–32in) apart. You can experiment with this spacing by marking out where each foot falls at your own natural pace.

It is difficult to make any stepping-stone path without the walker having to be aware of where their feet land, but if you make the joints between them quite tight, no more than 10cm (4in), and level with the height of the stone, the transition between each will be easier. Most stepping-stone paths are placed higher than the

Below: Small stepping stones sunk in a carpet of moss wander through this private garden in Ohara. The small symbolic "lantern" by the tree is made of stones piled up on top of each other.

surrounding soil, but this will depend on how thick your stepping stones are. You may find it difficult to obtain random stones of the quality and thickness that you could find in Japan. The use of substitutes such as logs, or concrete logs with strips of bamboo, is fine as long as you keep them clean of slimy algae. All stepping stones, especially those that are sawn rather than riven, can become slippery, especially in shady gardens, so be prepared to clean them occasionally to reduce their slipperiness.

Path styles

To the Japanese, a path is not simply a way of moving around the garden without getting your shoes muddy – it is a precisely designed element of the garden that directs you to certain points, where the view is carefully constructed to be seen from that point. A path can be of great spiritual significance, as in the stepping-stone paths of the tea garden, symbolizing the progress of the spiritual seeker. There are three specific styles of path used by the Japanese: informal (*so*) paths, semi-formal (*gyo*) paths and formal (*shin*) paths.

Above: *This* shin *path uses formal paving blocks that are combined with a formal pattern. Moss is used to link the two elements.*

INFORMAL AND FORMAL STYLES

Around the turn of the 17th century there was a movement away from pure naturalism in the use of stone paths, and towards a greater emphasis on the design element. A greater freedom of expression allowed designers to use a variety of materials and patterns and to exhibit more formalism. While the original tea paths were laid out with a series of informal stepping stones, natural slabs of stone or buried boulders, later paths tended to blend in more formal shapes.

The Japanese expressions for the varying styles of path are *so* (informal), *gyo* (semi-formal) and *shin* (formal). This was linked to a social means of determining the level of formality for greeting people of varying status.

Stepping-stone paths were designed to unite separate parts of a garden, areas often with different atmospheres. The path may start near to the house, being set with formal paving or cobbling, and then launch off across a sea of sand before entering a more earthy and mossy "forest" area planted with maples and shrubs. In each case a different style of paving can be used.

Informal (*so*) paths

These are paths that may be made of rough, uncut stepping stones set in a weaving motion. It also applies to straight paths made up of random stones, without well-defined edges.

Semi-formal (*gyo*) paths

This mixing of the rough with the smooth, the informal with the formal, can be expressed in different ways. Square stepping stones can be set in the

Left: *An interrupted line of formal rectangular granite slabs helps to contain a* gyo *path of mixed natural cobbles and stones.*

Above: *These formal paving stones combine with an informal surround of other stones.*

Above: *This gyo path through a rock garden uses formal materials in an informal pattern.*

Above: *A so path through a bamboo grove uses informal materials and an informal pattern.*

same weaving motion as rough uncut stepping stones, but being of a formal shape they will give a different impression. Rectangular or square paving set out in this manner could flow through planted areas or across areas of moss or a sea of sand. Another mixture might use informal random stones bordered by straight-edged granite setts or long strips of paving. Other semi-formal paths might have square forms with sections of informal cobbles, roofing tiles set on edge and natural paving. The use of old roof tiles, mill stones and reclaimed relics is seen as a sign of good taste.

Formal (*shin*) paths

These paths may be made of square paving, bordered by long, rectangular granite setts, or paved in random but rectilinear patterns. This kind of path will look quite familiar to the Western gardener as it is commonly used in terraces, patios and driveways.

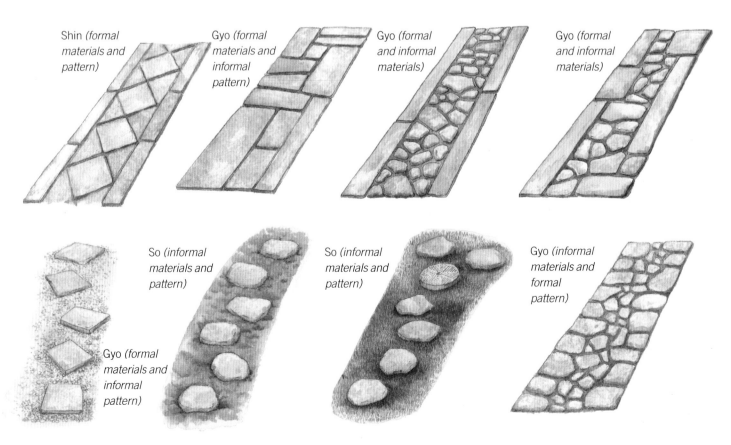

Shin *(formal materials and pattern)*

Gyo *(formal materials and informal pattern)*

Gyo *(formal and informal materials)*

Gyo *(formal and informal materials)*

Gyo *(formal materials and informal pattern)*

So *(informal materials and pattern)*

So *(informal materials and pattern)*

Gyo *(informal materials and formal pattern)*

Tea houses & other buildings

Early Japanese gardens had Chinese-style viewing pavilions, designed to give a view of the pond and garden, often built at the end of a long covered corridor that was open to the sides. The introduction in the 16th century of the unique Japanese tea house would come to influence the style and character of Japanese garden buildings to the present day. Apart from the traditional tea house, other buildings can also be a feature of the Japanese garden, such as small pavilions and arbours surrounded by plants with a place to sit and look at the view.

Above: *Wisteria-covered arbours are popular in Japanese gardens. They are simple constructions of robust timbers to carry the weighty stems of wisteria, with very little, if any, ornamentation.*

THE JAPANESE TEA HOUSE

The tea house was originally conceived by the Japanese as "a mountain place in the city", and it was often built as a rustic hut that was thatched with grass, but later became increasingly sophisticated in design. Originally, the tea house was the place to which the tea garden path led, and it was a place of reverence and social intercourse; it was not a place from which to view the garden. However, by the 17th century, especially in the exquisite gardens of the Katsura Palace in Kyoto, the tea house had opened up its sides and front so that its visitors could look out over the new pond and stroll gardens.

If you want to build a tea house in your garden, then you can easily create a structure that can be used as an outdoor room, but still retains the key elements of the ancient style. Paying close attention to the design of the building and the materials will give your tea house an undeniable air of authenticity.

TEA HOUSE COMPONENTS

All the materials you might need to build a tea house are readily available. The main elements are:

• a mixture of natural raw materials blended with finely planed, high-quality timber;

• a floor consisting of a layer of straw mats (tatami) bordered by fabric;

• the supports for the buildings might be made using the whole trunks of small trees with the bark left on;

• the walls are often finished with plaster, lined with bamboo strips, or painted in weathered gold and pale blue.

Left: *This unusual tea house was shipped from Japan to the English garden of Heale House in the early 1900s, where it stands on stone pillars so that it can straddle a stream.*

TEA HOUSE INTERIORS

The essential elements of tea house interiors typically include the entrance hatch, which in 16th-century tea houses was a small 76cm (2½ft) square sliding-door hatch, so that guests were forced to enter on their knees and demonstrate a suitable level of respect for the ceremony to come. Other window-like openings are often round, like the moon, or rectilinear with sliding rice-paper panels. There is often a sunken hearth for heating the tea water, which is placed off-centre. Calligraphic scrolls might hang in a special alcove (*tokonoma*) in the back wall. There might also be a vase containing a simple, seasonal, "country-style" flower arrangement.

You may not wish to go to the trouble of building a sunken hearth in your tea house, but even if you are simply using the tea house as an outdoor shelter or gazebo, you might still include some classic Japanese design features to give the structure an air of authenticity. There is nothing ostentatious whatsoever about these tea houses, and they blend beautifully into the landscape.

OTHER BUILDINGS

Different types of building might include a small open-fronted waiting room, similar to a rustic shelter with benches, where guests can relax before being invited by the host to proceed to the tea house. There might also be outside toilets for a tea garden built in a similar style to that of the tea house. Raised boarded walkways are also common in stroll gardens, used for viewing the cherry blossom, and these could lead to a thatched pavilion. You might find umbrella-shaped arbours, with a single pillar supporting a circular or square thatched roof, for viewing the garden, or Chinese-style hexagonal shelters, similar to modern Western gazebos. In and around such a shelter were often portable benches and tables, some in the style of Chinese porcelain tubs. These arbours and pavilions are often placed in more prominent places than tea houses, such as on a hill crest or other vantage point.

In some ancient gardens, the contrast of bright red paper umbrellas over tables draped in red cloth, set against dark green evergreen trees and shrubs, can be quite startling, an approach that would even suit a contemporary Japanese garden.

Above right: The waiting room alongside the tea path is often of the simplest design, such as this one at Newstead Abbey, England.

Right: A Japanese tea house gets an English touch in the form of a wicker chair. The Japanese usually sit directly on tatami mats.

Far right: The interior of a tea house at Toji-in. The materials are natural and simple, but the craftsmanship is detailed and refined.

Boundaries

Ever since Heian times (794–1185), when the city of Kyoto was laid out on a strict grid system, Japanese gardens have invariably had distinctive boundaries. This approach did not really change until the Edo period (1603–1867), when gardens became large enough for their perimeters to be of secondary importance to the overall design. Now that the average garden is fairly small, the walls, fences and hedges have once again become an important element in the design, and are made to be admired.

WALLS

The outer boundary walls of large houses and temple gardens that were constructed before the Edo period were designed as a reflection of the architecture of the buildings. They also became an important backdrop and could be seen from within the garden. These boundary walls were often built of clay and tiles, and were usually neatly plastered. With a stout wooden framework and bracket as a cornice, they were usually crowned with ornamental tiling, although they were sometimes thatched on the top with a ridge of protective tiles.

These walls were rather grand structures, suited to palaces and temples, but smaller residences used many of the same techniques and materials. Modern brick and stone were used more rarely in traditional Japanese gardens, although many garden boundaries on slopes were supported by stone retaining walls, sometimes with azaleas growing in their crevices. Incidentally, internal walls around courtyards were often kept lower than perimeter walls, giving views of trees or distant hills.

Walls in Japanese gardens tend not to be used for growing exotic plants or fruits, as they are in Western gardens. When climbing plants are grown, in large and small gardens, they are allowed to twine through light bamboo trellising.

If you would like to give a Japanese look to conventional brick or concrete block walls, including walls around a courtyard or Zen-style dry garden, the careful use of plaster, paint and some timber uprights at intervals can be effective. Top with large reclaimed or new terracotta pantiles for an authentic finish.

FENCES

Beyond the practicalities of privacy and security, fences were, and still are, considered an important garden feature. In the use of bamboo, in particular, the Japanese have excelled in their inventiveness. An ornate bamboo fence may be woven into wonderful patterns,

Left: *The wall surrounding the garden amid the sweeping roofs of the temple of Tofuku-ji is an intrinsic part of the overall design, with its vertical blackened timber supports and heavily tiled coping.*

Above: *The use of vertical boarding is generally seen as aesthetically the most pleasing and is very practical when changes of ground level require adjustments in the levels of a wall or fence.*

Left: *Vertical bands of reeds seem to mimic the trunks of the trees in this elegant bamboo fence found in the Nanzen-in temple, in Kyoto. The use of raw natural materials such as unpainted wood or bamboo allows a boundary fence to merge with the trees beyond.*

Below: *Horizontal bands of split bamboo, tied to the main fence with black jute, add strength and beauty to this fence. The Japanese use these bands to create many different designs.*

bundled together, tied with jute, or combined with branches, twigs, thatch or bundles of reeds, to flow alongside a path or to help direct the way.

Generally, timber fences are left raw and unpainted. At their most rustic, planks might be old and weathered or sometimes deliberately chiselled and charred to give an instantly distressed and aged effect.

A hybrid between a fence and a wall is the wattle-and-daub fence. The upright support timbers are often left exposed and stained black. Posts with horizontal, vertical or even angled boarding are also used, sometimes with the boards staggered to allow air and light through and occasionally with gaps that are wide enough to allow visitors to peep out.

Japanese bamboo fences can be expensive to buy or build but you can make suitable and more affordable fences using simple methods. Try rolls of bamboo tied to posts, and add superficial framing with other materials such as timber or pine. If you are unable to find authentic fencing for a traditional Japanese tea garden or pond garden, you can use willow or hazel hurdles, chestnut paling or rustic pole fencing. These alternative fencing materials are usually available from larger garden centres and fencing specialists, the latter often providing an on-site construction service if you require it.

SLEEVE FENCES (*SODE-GAKI*)

These are screens of bamboo and reeds that were, and still are, used for two reasons: firstly to deflect the view to another part of the garden, and secondly to create privacy. This is often the case in Japanese restaurants, where guests do not want to be aware of other diners, yet still wish to have a view of the garden, usually a courtyard (*tsuboniwa*). Sleeve fences are usually about 2m (6½ft) high by 1m (1yd) wide, often curved at shoulder level and pierced by an aperture. They come in different designs, from rustic to more formal, and work well in modern gardens.

Above: *A granite water basin and an artificial bamboo fence constructed in a fan shape with jute ties. There is also a Donald Duck figure, a popular feature in contemporary Japan.*

Below: *This main entrance gate to the Huntington Botanical Gardens needs to be secure so is built of more substantial materials such as timber and roofing tiles.*

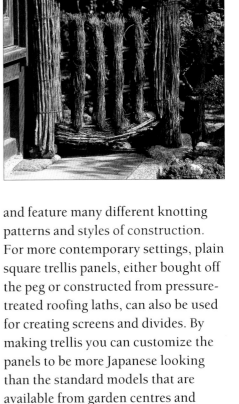

Above: *Sleeve fences are a classic feature used to frame a view.*

Above right: *A bamboo panel tied with jute is framed between two branches. At the step, guests remove their shoes before entering the tea house.*

Above far right: *Brushwood, reeds and bamboo are combined in this sleeve fence.*

Below right: *These bamboo fence posts tied with jute give a dense, yet informal, barrier to this entrance gateway.*

TREATING NATURAL MATERIALS

The Japanese tend to leave fences unpainted to retain their natural look:

• achieve a blackened effect with several coats of dark wood stain;

• treat the base of posts that go into the ground with wood preservative;

• bamboo fences last longer painted with a layer of matt varnish diluted with white spirit;

• wooden fences can be preserved using linseed oil or oil-based stains.

SCREENS

Western-style brick walls, fence panels, wooden sheds and outbuildings can be camouflaged or blended into your Japanese garden by fixing on bamboo roll or other screening materials such as the darker, more rustic-looking heather screening. Rigid panels, made of framed sections of split bamboo, heather or willow, are also available to conceal pre-existing buildings.

Traditional Japanese screens, including curved sleeve or wing panels, come in a wide variety of designs made from bamboo or brushwood and feature many different knotting patterns and styles of construction. For more contemporary settings, plain square trellis panels, either bought off the peg or constructed from pressure-treated roofing laths, can also be used for creating screens and divides. By making trellis you can customize the panels to be more Japanese looking than the standard models that are available from garden centres and fencing specialists. Paint or stain them black and, for privacy, attach bamboo, heather or brushwood roll to the back using an industrial staple gun.

Left: *Zigzagging down the hill, this bamboo post and rail fence helps to emphasize the garden's contours.*

Except perhaps in the case of contemporary Japanese gardens, one desirable feature is that any constructions look attractively weathered even when relatively new. Though bamboo tends to take a couple of years to fade and lose its sheen, after washing and rubbing down it can be treated with stains, oils, waxes or varnish as required. Bamboo can also be effectively "aged" and blackened using a gas blowtorch.

HEDGES

Japanese box hedges (*Buxus microphylla*), evergreen oak (*Quercus ilex*), Japanese cedar (*Cryptomeria*), photinia and podocarpus are common. Where they thin near their base, they may be backed by bamboo fencing.

Japanese hedges are almost always evergreen, so plant a mixture for a varied texture. Camellias and other flowering plants can be used, especially the autumn-flowering *Camellia sasanqua*.

WATER AND PATH EDGINGS

Although on a smaller scale, these boundaries are also important in the Japanese garden, both practically and aesthetically. Water features and pathways will always benefit from neat but natural-looking edging. This approach is practical too, as a firm edge will help to retain and strengthen pond banks and define areas of gravel and other loose material. If you are making pond edgings, or outlining paths and raised beds, use lines of tanalized or pressure-treated logs or rounded posts set in a bed of concrete to hold them rigid. The advantage of this approach is that this edging is 100 per cent flexible, creating curves and following the rise and fall of the land as required.

GATES

Often at the main entrance to the garden, the gate is the threshold between the busy outside world and the calm and tranquil mood of the garden beyond.

The entry gate to a Japanese garden is often a low wooden structure with a roof. This has a humbling effect reminding visitors of their stature in comparison with the space they are about to enter. It may be simply an opening in the wall or fence or a hinged structure often made from latticed bamboo. Particular attention is given to the floor of the entry gate. Stones are carefully selected for this area and positioned with much care.

A classic *Torii* gate, consisting of two vertical posts joined with a double crossbar and often painted red, may be used to indicate that you are entering a sacred space.

Left: *This entrance is flanked by sections of traditional Japanese bamboo fencing, which is lashed together with black twine. This see-through fencing style blends in well with the natural surroundings.*

Gates were very popular in tea gardens, developing their most elaborate and ritualistic style by the early 17th century. The traditional tea garden is often divided into two or even three parts: an inner, middle and outer garden, linked by a *roji* (dewy path), featuring specially designed gates opening into each area.

The main entrance gate (*roji-mon*) may be a large tile-covered gatehouse or a simple thatch-covered bamboo gate. The second gate into the middle or inner *roji* might be a small crawl-through opening or stooping gate (*naka-kuguri*). One type has a door that is hinged at the top so that the guest has to push it forward and up to get through, being forced to bow in the process. This can be propped open.

You can simulate this effect with a series of sections, each with their own entrance, to enhance the feeling of deference as you approach the tea house, and give the garden authenticity.

You can buy ready-made Japanese gates, or make your own from natural materials, using a simple shape hinged at the side or top.

Right: *This gateway, with its thatched roof, is a symbolic statement as well as a physical entrance to the tea garden at Nijo castle. Such roofs can also be finished with wooden shingles.*

READY-MADE STRUCTURES

A wide range of traditional Japanese structures are available direct from Japan or through specialist importers. These include garden screens, fence panels and roofed gateways. Details can be found on the internet, through mail order firms advertising in specialist directories and in the classified sections of home and garden magazines.

In addition, a number of companies outside Japan manufacture structures either to catalogue specifications or as bespoke items. The best of these use traditional materials and methods such as split bamboo and black hemp for tying and knotting.

DO IT YOURSELF

If you like the idea of having your own construction project, build or adapt screens, fences and walls using a variety of raw materials. There are mail order and internet supply companies selling the basic materials, from bamboo poles to lengths of split bamboo and wooden roof shingles.

Making a tea-path gate

Small lattice bamboo gates are very lightweight and are easy to install. Gates are very common features throughout Japanese gardens, from the main entrance to key points within the garden or along the tea path. The gates that are sited on the tea path itself are often not meant to keep people or animals out of the garden, but are more of a symbolic feature, for example the middle crawl-through gate. In the case of the tea-path gate, it is quite usual for the gate to be found standing alone with no fence on either side of it.

The simple design of this gate gives the garden an airy feel, especially when associated with live bamboo plants, maples and glossy evergreens, the kind of plants that you would find in a tea garden.

This system for hanging a gate is only suitable for very lightweight gates that are made of bamboo or light wood, as we have used light posts and heavy twine for the top hinge. For heavier gates, you will need to use stronger posts and a hinge at both top and bottom, but the methods of measuring and levelling will be the same. This bamboo gate is also hinged in such a way that gravity will ensure that the gate naturally swings to a close behind you.

Above: *The semi-transparent nature of this jute-tied bamboo trellis gate gives a light and airy feel to a garden.*

As the gate is merely symbolic and not designed to be child or animal safe there is no latch, but a loop of twine could easily be attached to the top of the gate to keep it firmly shut.

You will need
- a lightweight lattice bamboo gate
- 2 x 7.5cm (3in) round softwood gateposts, ideally pressure treated or with wood preservative on the base
- an L-shaped gate hinge with a pin that will fit inside the bamboo frame
- a short length of black jute or nylon rope
- a hammer
- a crowbar
- a small sledgehammer
- a spirit level
- a hand saw
- dark ash black wood stain and a paintbrush (optional)
- an electric drill or hand wood drill

1 Having chosen the site, you must decide which way the gate will open and on which side the hinge should be. Now make the first hole for the post that the gate will hang on. This needs to be deeper than the "receiving" post. Prepare the hole with a crowbar, to a depth of at least 30cm (12in).

2 Prepare both posts for the gate by staining them, if you like, and making sure that the part below the ground is protected with wood preservative. Place the hinge post in the hole and check by eye that it is more or less vertical. If you have an assistant, ask them to hold the hinge post while you knock it into the ground with a sledgehammer. It is a good idea to protect the top of the post with a block of wood to prevent the top of the post from being damaged by the sledgehammer.

3 Using a spirit level, check that the post is upright. Check the distance to the other post by laying the gate in place. The receiving post can be at a slighter narrower width than the gate so that the gate will lean against it when closed. Prepare the second post hole with the crowbar and knock in the receiving post.

4 It is better that your posts are set a little too high, so that you can cut them off to the right height. The tops of the posts should line up with the top of the gate or can be slightly higher. Using a spirit level, check that the two posts are level with each other. If they need to be cut, mark the cutting line.

5 Cut off the tops of the posts with a wood saw if necessary to ensure they are level. If you have stained the post to give it the blackened and charred look that the Japanese love to create, you will need to paint some more wood stain on to the cut surface at the top.

6 Check the height of the gate against the post, positioning it so that the bottom of the gate will hang just off the ground, clearing any stones or paving slabs. Mark on the hinge post where the bottom hinge needs to be.

7 Select a drill-bit slightly smaller than the diameter of the hinge. Drill to the depth needed. Alternatively you can buy a hinge with a flat plate that can be drilled directly on to the side of the post.

8 Knock the hinge in firmly with a hammer. Drop the gate on to the hinge and tie a piece of black jute in a figure of eight around the post near the top. You may need to adjust this until the gate hangs and swings comfortably.

9 The gate can now swing until it just touches the side of the receiving post. If the gate hangs well, you may not need to secure it, but another loop of jute could be used to secure the gate to the receiving post.

Right: *The gate acts as a transition into the inner* roji *of a tea garden with its* tsukubai *arrangement of lantern and water basin.*

Bridges

Always a dominant feature, bridges tend to be particularly associated with Japanese gardens. One of the most well known is the Chinese-style bridge (*sori-hashi*), lavishly ornamented, high-arched and lacquered red or orange. While the islands in a pond represented the abodes of the immortals, bridges symbolized the crossing over to that world. These red-painted bridges are often closely associated with Japanese gardens in the Western mind, but they are in fact rarer in authentic designs than those made of more natural materials and unpainted wood.

Above: *A moss-covered log bridge in the gardens of Saiho-ji, the Moss Temple in Kyoto, where over 60 species of moss are said to grow.*

STYLES OF BRIDGE

In the garden of the Tenryu-ji, built in the 14th century, a Chinese-style, curved red wooden bridge was replaced by a series of flat, natural stone slabs, propped up on rock pillars. Later gardens used single pieces of wrought granite, supported by granite piles. Some of these granite slabs were carved with a gentle curve. This was the dominant style of Japanese bridges until Chinese high-arched bridges returned to favour in the Edo period (1603–1867). These semicircular bridges, known as full-moon bridges because their reflections in the water make up a complete circle, are so steep that the only way to cross over them is by means of steps going up one side and down the other.

YATSUHASHI BRIDGES

Especially designed for viewing iris beds, the *yatsuhashi* style of bridge, which is still popular today, is constructed from a series of single horizontal planks, which are supported by short wooden piles that are driven into the mud at the head of the pond, where the Japanese love to grow beds of irises. The planks cross the swampy beds in a zigzag fashion, forcing the visitor to loiter, watch the fish and admire the flowers. This simple style of bridge can easily be incorporated into today's Japanese garden, perhaps designed to sit in a boggy area in which moisture-loving plants such as irises and sedges can be grown. See overleaf for instructions for making a *yatsuhashi* bridge.

WATTLE AND LOG BRIDGES

Bridges were also often made from wattle (woven branches) then covered in earth, or from batches of logs bundled and laid across a timber frame and then covered with earth and gravel. These were designed more for effect because they were fairly fragile, and did not usually feature a hand-rail. Those that link up the islands at the famous Moss Temple, in Kyoto, for example, are quite rotten, but they blend in with the deep shady mystery of the garden. If you want to construct this type of bridge, consider how long you want it to last and whether the logs should be treated in order to improve their longevity. Nowadays, wattle is not easily available, so it is best to use bundles of logs that have been coated in a wood preservative, or use a good hardwood, such as oak, which needs no treatment.

WISTERIA BRIDGES

Sturdy wooden bridges with a trellised canopy to carry twining wisterias are popular in Japan. This style of bridge was immortalized by Monet in his

Left: *This style of red-painted bridge, seen here in the gardens at Heale House in England, is Chinese in origin, and became popular in Japan in the Edo period.*

paintings of his garden at Giverny, in France. The effect of the long racemes of the Japanese wisteria (*Wisteria floribunda*) is doubled when they are reflected in the water, and cascades of wisteria flowers create a shady, scented walkway to stroll on.

STEPPING-STONE BRIDGES

These bridges can be made of recycled pillars or natural rocks. Like the *yatsuhashi*, the stones zigzag across the water instead of taking a straight line, offering a variety of views as you cross streams, inlets and ponds, and possibly echoing the wandering nature of the path it joins at either end. If you

are lucky enough to have a large garden with an expanse of water, a stepping-stone bridge would make a delightful feature.

Top: *This massive curving slab of schist in the grounds of Nijo castle is a symbol of strength. The original garden was thought to have been designed as a dry garden with no water at all.*

Above: *Another style of bridge, borrowed from China. The high arch allows the passage of boats underneath but the sides are so steep they require steps to cross over them.*

Right: *This stepping-stone bridge in the garden of Tenju-an is made of unusually shaped piers – possibly recycled temple-pillar bases.*

Making a *yatsuhashi* bridge

The *yatsuhashi* bridge is a popular form in Japanese gardens. The origin of the name *yatsuhashi* is a poetic reference to a timber bridge made of eight planks that zigzag across a river. The idea is to delight the eye of visitors to the garden with unexpected sights as they make their way over the bridge and across a pond or swampy area filled with flowers. It should also encourage them to linger and admire an unexpected aspect of the garden. A *yatsuhashi* bridge is relatively simple to construct, as it requires only a few posts and planks.

This unique kind of bridge is mostly found in gardens where the inlet of a stream flows into a pond, or any other area that is similarly ideal for the growing of the Japanese water iris (*Iris ensata*). *Yatsuhashi* bridges do not have to have eight planks – they can be made up of as few as two planks, and whatever their size, they are an excellent addition to any small or large pond or stroll gardens. In some cases the device can simply be a design that is viewed but not actually used to walk on.

When constructing the bridge, make sure that your measurements are accurate, so the planks will be level. If possible, drain the pond water first.

Above: *Although appearing to be complex in design, the actual construction of a* yatsuhashi *bridge is relatively simple.*

If you cannot drain the pond or other water feature, it is still possible to construct a bridge but you may need to get professional help as setting the posts into water can present problems.

You will need

- planks or boards at least 5cm (2in) thick – the number and length of planks and posts will be determined by the span and depth of water you are working with, and the width of the planks can also be variable
- supporting posts, 7.5cm (3in) square or round
- cross beams, 7.5cm (3in) deep x 5cm (2in) thick – the length of these will be determined by the width of the planks
- bolts, minimum 1cm (⅜in) wide by 15cm (6in) long
- an electric drill with wood bits
- cement and concreting sand/aggregate
- metal post holders (for a butyl-lined pond)
- a shovel
- a spade
- a crowbar
- a coarse-toothed wood-saw
- a sledgehammer if you are driving posts into the ground or a clay-lined pond

POSITIONING YOUR BRIDGE

When considering the design of your *yatsuhashi* bridge, use the angles to encourage the garden visitor to take in varying views. You may even place a bench at a strategic position on the bridge.

1 Measure the exact span for the bridge and make a sketch of how many planks will be needed to cross your inlet, iris bed or pond, and the length of the planks. The directional changes do not have to be at 90 degrees – they can be at even sharper angles.

2 Measure how deep the water is at different points to calculate how many posts you need and how long they should be.

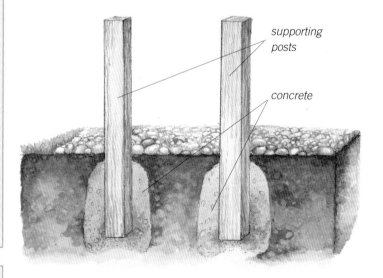

supporting posts

concrete

3 Start on dry land by setting two posts in the ground exactly the width of one plank apart, or two plank widths if you are laying two planks side by side. The posts need to be dug into the ground to a depth of 45–60cm (18–24in) and their bases set in two or three shovelfuls of concrete (1 part cement to 6 parts concreting sand or aggregate). If the first set of posts will be in the water, follow step 7 opposite.

Timber bearer/
cross beam

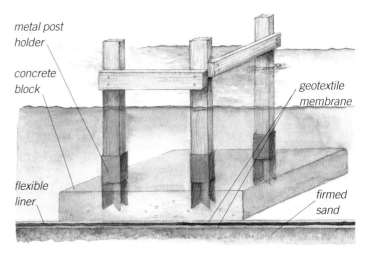

metal post
holder

concrete
block

geotextile
membrane

flexible
liner

firmed
sand

4 Measure how high you want the bridge to be off the ground and make a mark on one of the posts. With a spirit level, mark across to the other post. Attach the cross beam on to the posts using bolts. Stout screws may suffice but bolts will be stronger and last longer. The first set of planks may overlap these first posts by up to 30cm (12in).

5 Drain off the water if possible, as this makes it much easier to construct the bridge. Driving posts into the clay base or mixing cement directly into water is very tricky and unreliable.

6 Measure across to where the next set of posts will stand. The first set of planks will overlap the second set of posts by the width of a plank, as the next set of planks will lie over the top of the first.

7 The second set of posts may be dug or driven directly into the base of a clay-lined pool, but in a pool with a butyl liner, they will need to sit in post holders and be set in a concrete base (1 part cement to 5 parts concreting sand). You can use fast-setting concrete that is specially designed for posts and will set in less than 15 minutes.

8 Leave the concrete to set for at least a day before laying the planks and two days before you walk on them. You only need three posts at each junction, but four will make the bridge more stable. If you prefer the look of three posts, include a fourth one for strength and trim it off flush to the top of the cross beam. Attach cross beams as in step 4 and continue one set of posts at a time, testing them for measurements as you go. On the far side you may need another pair of posts on dry land.

Below: *A* yatsuhashi *bridge of planks, resting on wooden piles, staggers past baskets of irises towards an impressive stand of cycads.*

Decorative artefacts

The addition of objects without any useful function is generally avoided in Japanese gardens. The garden is regarded as a completely integrated composition, and the introduction of unnecessary features can destroy the unity of the design. Many Japanese garden designs are either inspired by nature or reproduce famous views; they avoid distractions that might divert the eye from reading the composition as a whole. However, the useful objects such as water basins and lanterns that are found in gardens can be beautiful in their own right.

Above: *A pagoda stands in the middle of an island in the gardens of the Golden Pavilion (Kinkaku-ji), in Kyoto.*

In the Japanese garden, specimen plants, focal points, sculptures and statues are usually shunned, as are overt colour schemes, textural combinations, surprise effects and most of the elements that are the bedrock of many Western gardens.

This general emphasis still accommodates the more focused effect of sculptural forms with a religious connotation. These include garden stupas, pagodas, water basins, lanterns, or images of the Buddha. Although these artefacts are still

integral to modern Japanese gardens, their religious significance can be more diluted.

PAGODAS AND STUPAS

These are structures of the Buddhist treasure houses where relics and scriptures were stored to commemorate a saint. Like lanterns, they were found close to temples, but when used in the garden they do not dominate because they are such familiar images that they readily blend into the scene. Indeed, both pagodas and stupas represent very recognizable features, from a Western viewpoint, of the Japanese garden and what it should contain.

WATER DEVICES

There are one or two playful devices found in Japanese gardens that recall a distant rural past. Deer scarers (*shishi-odoshi*) are the best known of these. They use water to make a noise intended to startle any deer feeding on plants in the garden (see page 120). A more unusual device is the *sui-kinkutsu* (see page 121). It literally

Left: *Carved reliefs and sculptures of the Buddha are sometimes placed in gardens, as many gardens are inspired by the philosophy of Zen Buddhism.*

means "water harp chamber" and distills the sound of water dripping in an underground chamber.

Wells may also be found in Japanese gardens, constructed of timber or natural stone, and often with a bamboo rack as a cover to prevent leaves from falling in. The use of wells, whether real or decorative, is common in conjunction with tea gardens to indicate a pure source of water for making tea.

Left: *A stone pagoda stands in a grove of the rare Chinese fir (*Cunninghamia lanceolata*) in the stroll garden of Syoko-ho-en, Kyoto.*

Above: *This water mill, sited in the gardens of the Nijo castle in Kyoto, has been decorated to become a feature.*

Below left: *Kasuga, temple-style lanterns are very impressive and can be very large, often standing over 2m (7ft) high.*

Below: *Wells are often found in tea gardens, with a stone at the side for the water bucket. Many, such as this one, are purely ornamental.*

Lighting

There is a large selection of garden lights available, from tiny concealed uplighters made to highlight individual plants or rocks, to Japanese-style lanterns, which are among the most distinctive sculptural artefacts in the Japanese garden. Originally these lanterns stood outside Shinto shrines and Buddhist temples, sometimes in their hundreds, lining up in avenues of flickering lights. On a more practical level, lighting allows you to view the garden at night from the house rather like a painting. It also makes the garden usable at night and can create different moods.

LANTERNS IN THE TEA GARDEN

Like other artefacts such as the water basin and the stepping-stone path, lanterns found their way into the Japanese garden, by way of the tea garden. They were originally placed to illuminate tea paths and water basins, as many tea gatherings were arranged in the evening. They were also placed near pond edges to represent lighthouses, or at the base of slopes or near wells. Despite their popularity, stone lanterns (with oil and wick lamps or candles placed inside) did not give much light and were, to a large extent, ornamental.

Below: Lanterns in Japanese tea gardens have taken on numerous forms, from the large temple-like "Kasuga" lantern to small lanterns designed to look best when covered in snow.

THE WEATHERING PROCESS

Sculpted ornaments are rare in Japanese gardens, so stone lanterns, especially granite ones, give an opportunity to create something interesting and distinctive. Brand new granite lanterns are often bright silvery grey and the colour can be too startling. It can take many years before granite weathers naturally to give that patina or aged effect that is evoked in the term *wabi-sabi*. The term, with no literal translation, roughly means "withered loneliness" and became an essential part of the tea ceremony philosophy. When applied to ornaments, it implies the patina of age. So encourage your lanterns to discolour and grow algae, lichen and moss. The more porous sandstone lanterns weather more quickly.

Above: Cast-iron lanterns are hung from trees and verandas and are used less as part of the overall garden design than stone lanterns.

There are ways to speed up this process. One effective method is to smear a lantern with yogurt or manure (soak some manure in a bucket of water and just paint it on), promoting the growth of algae. Repeat this monthly for three months, especially in the autumn when it is damp. In summer, in hot exposed positions, algae and lichen will not take a hold so readily as in the cooler, wetter months. Some gardeners even used the slime of crushed snails to achieve dampness. Another method is to drape them in pine boughs for a month or two. Stone ages more quickly when placed in the shade.

Kasuga

Snow scene

Mile post

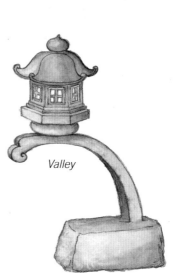

Valley

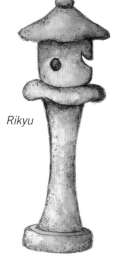

Rikyu

Above left: *Many temple-style lanterns still carry Buddhist motifs, such as this one crowned with a lotus bud.*

Above centre: *Organic rock forms can be layered on each other to create a lantern shape. These naturalistic forms can add an unusually animistic quality to a garden.*

Above right: *The valley lantern has been specially designed to place by the water's edge where the light from the lamp, usually an oil wick, can be seen to reflect in the water.*

Left: *The introduction of the stone lantern into Japanese gardens came through the development of the tea garden, where they were used to light the path (roji) and water basins.*

Below: *Short and stocky lanterns are often placed near water or at the end of gravel spits to evoke lighthouses.*

STYLES OF LANTERN

Lanterns play such a large part in Japanese gardens that long ago they were classified into different types. Some were named after famous tea masters or gardens; the most well known and popular of these is the Oribe lantern. Oribe was an eccentric samurai tea master active at the end of the 17th century. The Oribe lantern often has a Buddha carved on the front of the pillar base. In some gardens this image was disguised and purported to be of the Virgin Mary, an image that was banned after the Christian

Above: *There are many styles of Japanese stone lantern. This is a* kodal rokkaku.

Westerners were evicted from Japan in the 17th century. The Oribe lantern is easy to install. Taller and statuesque lanterns such as the Kasuga sit on a round plinth, some of them with elaborate carvings of lotus petals. More squat stone lanterns and low lanterns that rest on a tripod or four feet are often placed by the sides of ponds.

In gardens with ponds designed to include a symbolic reproduction of the Amanohashidate Peninsula, a famous scenic spot on the northern coast of Honshu, a lantern is usually placed at the gravelled promontory. This is a classic example of *shakkei*, a small-scale version of real scenes or objects. Some of these poolside lanterns are designed to look especially beautiful when covered in snow, a regular feature of the Japanese winter.

Although most lanterns are made of stone, some are also made of wood and thatched with reed. Hanging lanterns made of bronze are also popular and can easily be moved around, hung from a tree or simply placed on a rock.

TSUKUBAI ARRANGEMENTS

The most popular way to use lanterns is as part of a *tsukubai* water feature in tea gardens, a classic arrangement that

Above left: *In some Japanese gardens, lanterns are the only architectural artefacts to be found. Most are never lit, but this one is. Rice-paper panels diffuse the light from the lit oiled paper.*

Above: *Lanterns were often designed to look dramatic within the larger landscape – this one is majestically placed within a pond.*

consists of a lantern placed near a water basin, with one or two paving stones in a sea of gravel at the base, and surrounded by ferns, camellias and sedges. Versions of *tsukubai* arrangements can also be found in courtyard gardens or along passages that lead to the front doors of houses and restaurant entrances. These often include a backing piece of bamboo fence, a water basin, and a pine or maple tree to provide shade and promote the growth of moss.

CONTEMPORARY USE OF LIGHTING

In the Muromachi and Momoyama periods, special platforms and gardens were made for "viewing the moon". Moonlight was especially revered and was considered to be at its most moving when seen across a dry garden. These days in Kyoto, many of the most popular gardens are open during the autumn months at night, when artificial lighting is laid out to highlight the main buildings, the reflections of water and the autumn colours of the maples. Modern dry gardens can also be lit in a surprisingly adventurous manner.

As traditional lanterns give off very little light, in a contemporary Japanese garden electric lighting could be used effectively. Low-voltage and wattage systems that are cheap to install and run are ideal. Many of the traditional stone lanterns and other Japanese-style garden lights that you can buy today can be fitted with low-voltage electric light. Another way to supplement the meagre light is to hang bronze lanterns or hurricane lamps from trees or posts.

In naturalistic Japanese gardens, small black uplighters are used to light rocks, plants and ornamental features. Other kinds of low-level lighting can be installed to illuminate a pathway or steps, and in decked areas, small LED or halogen lights can be recessed into the wood to great effect. Low-voltage garden lighting sets running off a transformer are relatively easy to install. Not connected directly to the mains supply, the cabling can lie close to the surface and does not have to be buried in armoured ducting, though great care must be taken to hide the fittings and wires so that they are not visible during the day, as this would spoil the romantic effect. It is advisable to use an electrical contractor to install lighting projects, however, and you must fit residual current devices, or circuit breakers, as a safety measure.

Right: *A low-level wall light is discreet and effective. Such lights can be fitted to help light the way to a door or gate.*

Far right: *LED uplighters can be set into wooden decking or into pathways that are paved with setts.*

Care & maintenance

There is a curious ambiguity about the Japanese garden. As a first impression, one might think that maintaining a spread of gravel, a rock or two, a pine tree and a bamboo would require very little work. However, a dynamic Japanese garden, even on a small scale, carpeted with moss and planted with several trees and shrubs around a pond, can in fact involve a high level of maintenance. What is more, Japanese gardeners are meticulous in the way they keep their gardens, and pay extraordinary attention to small details such as training, staking and pruning.

Above: *Most tree work can be dangerous and should be carried out by professionals who have safety certificates and insurance.*

WEEDING

Japanese gardens do need regular weeding. Weed-suppressing matting and weedkillers could be used – but Japanese gardening is meant to be meditative and calming, and the process of weeding is therefore part of the experience.

Weeding tools

Some of the tools used in Japanese gardens are less well known in Western gardens. There are various small choppers and chisel-like planting tools for working between plants and rocks, and a right-angled, short-handled hoe or cultivation tool that is ideal for working in tight spaces. Hand scythes or sickles are used for controlling ground cover plants and for cutting grass in hard-to-reach places or on sloping sites that are unsuitable for lawnmowers. You can also use nylon-line trimmers.

PRUNING

In Japan, teams of professionals descend on public and private gardens once or twice a year to carry out the specialized job of pruning. Most shrubs and trees can be tackled in early to late autumn, but some plants, such as plums, require pruning immediately after flowering in the spring. Pruning is vital because plants in the Japanese garden are used for their structural qualities as well as the beauty of their flowers and foliage, and so their growth must be kept in check. Because Japanese gardens are often quite densely planted, you need to decide how much light should fall on the ground between shrubs to encourage the growth of moss, mondo grass or other ground cover plants. Too much light and some plants will burn in the sun; too much shade might stunt or kill plants, leaving the earth exposed.

Trees are pruned in Japan to achieve some very striking effects. They may be made to look older than they really are by encouraging a broad trunk supporting gnarled branches; or to imitate windswept or lightning-struck trees in the wild.

Other pruning techniques include the art of creating semi-spherical azaleas, shapes that are often combined with rocks and carefully pruned trees, such as a windswept pine. *Hako-zukuri* is a technique to create box shapes that complement and echo architectural elements within a garden.

Trimming and shaping tools

Japanese gardeners use a wide range of tools which are designed to shape, prune and clip shrubs and trees. For large hedges, or gardens with a large

Above: *The various Japanese pruning tools include secateurs, shears, topiary clippers, pruning saws and sharpeners.*

Above: *The Japanese walk carefully on mossy ground with soft-soled shoes and brush the autumn leaves with twig brooms (besoms).*

number of shrubs, non-traditional powered trimmers are the easiest option, but large-leaved plants such as camellias should be pruned by hand using secateurs (pruners) to avoid shredding the foliage. Small, shaped shrubs are also best trimmed by hand.

Many trimming tools are similar to those used in topiary. For example, as well as a range of standard anvil and bypass secateurs or pruners, there are also special long-bladed, narrow-nosed cutters that are used to shorten the new growth on pine trees and to thin the bundles of needles. This kind of tool is useful for precision shaping and trimming individual twigs in topiary.

Individual tree branches are often trained to achieve the desired shape and angle using bamboo canes and galvanized or plastic-coated training wire. You can use ladders to reach taller trees, but you may find long-handled or telescopic pruners, loppers and pruning saws useful with their longer reach.

Another essential tool for a Japanese garden containing large shrubs and small trees is a small pruning saw with a curved blade that folds or retracts into the handle for safe storage.

Shears with short blades and narrow noses are perfect for trimming over the rounded or flattened plates of cloud-pruned trees and shrubs and also for shaping azaleas and other evergreens such as box to resemble rounded boulders. For precise snipping and trimming of foliage on a smaller scale you can buy sprung one-handed cutters or "sheep shears". These are not suitable for extended use as they are heavy.

RAKING GRAVEL AND SAND

One of the most meditative practices in a Japanese garden is raking gravel or sand in a dry garden (*kare-sansui*). In temple gardens the rhythmic, focused motions of raking are still part of the spiritual practices of Zen monks. The softer and finer the texture of the sand, grit or gravel, the more frequently it will need raking.

Sourcing rakes

Used for making and maintaining patterns in grit and sand, rakes are not easy to get hold of. You can fashion a traditional Japanese rake from a row of dowel rods fitted into a block of wood. The tool must be able to fit between rocks and between rock groupings and pathways or boundaries. A wide rake may be unwieldy in a restricted area, but for a large, open expanse of sand, a bigger rake will cover the space more quickly. When making your own rake, adjust the size of the teeth or the thickness of the dowel rods and their spacing according to the grain diameter of sand or gravel. The larger the gravel, the wider the space required.

BRUSHING, SWEEPING AND TIDYING

Soft brushwood brooms or besoms made from bundled twigs are used to sweep sand into patterns. These brooms are also used to sweep debris and leaves off paths and mossy areas. You could use a powered leaf blower, but take great care not to disturb any raked or levelled areas of sand or grit.

You will also need to ensure that paths made of stepping stones are kept clean and free of moss and slimy algae.

OTHER TASKS

Other occasional maintenance work:
• the repair and re-binding of bamboo fences and gates.
• making or repairing tree supports.
• cutting ground cover plants. Some larger Japanese gardens have lawns, but the grass is coarse and cannot be mown too closely. Where spreading dwarf bamboos are used instead of grass, they will need shearing once or twice a year.
• maintaining water features. Unless you have a natural stream or spring, pump filters must be cleaned and pools dredged to prevent them from silting up and to keep the water clean and fresh.

Below: *A Buddhist monk rakes gravel into wavelike patterns in the Zen garden at Zuiho-in Temple in Kyoto.*

Glossary

Amida Buddha the form of the Buddha whose promise of a western Paradise influenced Heian-period garden makers.

Aminoshidate a long pine-clad peninsula on the north coast of Honshu, and one of the five most famous scenic spots in Japan, often symbolically reproduced in gardens.

Aware Lamenting the passing of things, a heightened awareness of fleeting beauty. An emotional attitude to the natural world that infected the sensibility of Heian courtiers.

Bakufu the military bureaucracies that acted for the emperor.

Carp stone a stone placed at the base of waterfalls to represent a leaping fish. Indicates the strivings of humanity.

Cha-niwa tea garden. Garden immediately around the tea house.

Cha-noyu the tea ceremony.

Chonin the merchant class, especially those who enjoyed a period of wealth during the Edo period but were forced to hide it. They made elaborate gardens inside their unobtrusive houses.

Chozubachi taller style of water basin, often placed where it can be reached from a veranda.

Confucius (d. 479 BC) Chinese sage who laid down principles and morals. These were especially popular during the Edo period when Buddhism waned.

Crane island (*tsuru-shima*) part of the Mystic isles myth. Cranes carried the immortals on their backs, and became symbols of longevity. The crane island is portrayed by rocks indicating long necks or an upheld wing.

Daimyo a lord who owned land.

Dyana meditation. The Sanskrit word that is at the root of the word Zen.

Edo period from 1603 to 1867, when the Tokugawa shogunate ruled Japan from its new capital in Edo, now Tokyo.

Eisai the Buddhist monk attributed with bringing both Zen Buddhism and the first successfully transplanted tea plants to Japan in the 13th century.

Enshu, Kabori 17th-century garden designer and town planner, whose plans set new standards for garden design, influencing the Katsura palace and many temple gardens.

Fuji-san, **Mount Fuji** ("san" means mountain) sacred mountain whose form can be reproduced symbolically in gardens.

Fuzei taste.

Genji, The Tales of highly influential novel of the Heian period, written by Murasaki Shikobu.

Geomancy Chinese system that brings together many beliefs as to how buildings, cities and gardens should be laid out relative to directions, colours and elements. Also applied in systems of government. Includes such principles as yin-yang and feng-shui.

Go-shintai Shinto term for an area that is considered to be the abode of the gods.

Heian period from 794 to 1185, marking the period from when a new capital was created in Kyoto until the shogunate moved its headquarters to Kamakura.

Hiei-san mountain overlooking Kyoto, views of which were coveted by garden designers. See *shakkei*.

Hojo the abbot's quarters in Zen temples, where most dry Zen gardens were laid out.

Horai the central island in the ancient Chinese myth of the Mystic Isles, often portrayed by a large upright rock.

Immortals inhabitants of the Mystic Isles who possessed the secret of the

Equisetum hyemale

elixir of eternal youth. Mystic Isles were constructed in pond gardens in the hope of luring the immortals to earth.

Ishe-tate-so the "rock-setting priests" of the 14th and 15th centuries, who designed the first *kare-sansui* or dry gardens.

Iwa-kura literally "boulder-seat". Shintoists believed rocks possessed spirits, and certain rocks were given the status of gods, a factor that may well have influenced the way rocks were used in Japanese gardens.

Kamakura period from 1185 to 1392, following the Heian period, when the shogunate moved its headquarters from Kyoto to Kamakura, south of modern-day Tokyo.

Kame-shima see Turtle islands.

Kami the Shinto term for gods.

Kare-sansui the dry landscape garden, where the element of water is represented by sand and gravel.

Kawara-mono the lowest caste in Japan, attributed with having helped to build *kare-sansui* dry gardens during the Muromachi period, especially Ryoan-ji.

Koan Zen riddle to aid emptiness of mind, and a trigger for enlightenment.

Kyoto the most important capital city in the history of Japanese garden design.

Machiya smaller town houses belonging to merchants, which contained small *tsubo-niwa* or courtyard gardens.

Mappo the Buddhist age of "ending law" said to have started in the 11th century. The last of three ages predicted by the Buddha, inducing a sense of pessimism.

Matsushima pine-clad islands off the north-east coast of Japan that inspired reproduction in many gardens.

Meiji restoration the restoration of the emperor as acting head of state in 1868, and the end of the shogunate rule. The emperor moved to the new capital of Tokyo.

Mitate recycled second-hand building materials, such as millstones, incorporated into garden paths and buildings, which show the refined taste of their owner.

Prunus mume

Momoyama period from 1568 to 1603. The era of the generals, especially Totomi Hideyoshi, who unified Japan. The last of the generals was Ieyasu Tokugawa, whose family ruled throughout the Edo period.

Mu nothingness. An aspect of Zen that reveals itself in the empty spaces of sand in some dry Zen gardens.

Muromachi period from 1393 to 1568, when the shogunate returned from Kamakura to Kyoto. Possibly the most intensely creative period in Japanese history, which saw both the dry *kare-sansui* gardens and tea gardens come of age.

Mystic Isles see Horai, Crane island and Turtle island.

Naka-kuguri literally a middle crawl-through gate or stooping gate, a gate that deliberately induced a sense of humility along the tea path before a guest entered the tea house.

Nara period from 710 to 795. Nara was the last of the ancient capitals, standing 50 miles south of Kyoto, before a new capital was built in Kyoto.

Nigiriguchi a small hatch-like entrance to the tea house, whereby the guest entered on hands and knees.

No-da-te an informal tea ceremony conducted outdoors.

O-karikomi the Japanese form of topiary, where plants of many kinds are clipped into abstract shapes.

Pagoda a Japanese or Chinese building that contained relics of the Buddha or his saints. These were often symbolically carved in stone and placed in gardens.

Peng-lai original name for Mount Horai.

Pure Land paradise thought to be in the West, this was the Buddha's abode for the afterlife. Ponds were made to evoke this paradise, especially in the Heian and Kamakura periods.

Rikyu Japan's most famous tea-master, whose influence on the tea ceremony and tea garden is still felt today.

Roji literally "dewy path", the tea path that leads to the tea house.

Roji-mon the entrance gate to the tea garden or roji.

Ryoan-ji the most famous of all the dry Zen gardens in Kyoto, believed to have been built in 1499.

Sakuteiki the first and most influential garden treatise, which was written in the 11th century.

Samurai a soldier in service of a lord (*daimyo*).

Sanzon Buddhist trinity stone arrangements

Sesshu the most influential of Japanese brush and ink painters during the 15th century, who was also a gardener and a Zen priest.

Shakkei literally "borrowed landscape". The inclusion of distant views to become part of the garden scene.

Shibumi is derived from the word meaning "astringent". It describes the minimalist, unpretentious worldly aesthetic of the Edo period that replaced the earlier and more spiritual term *wabi-sabi*.

Shigemori, Mirei the most influential and celebrated Japanese garden designer of the 20th century.

Shiki-no-himorogi sacred areas covered with pebbles.

Shime the binding of artefacts, rocks and trees as part of the Shinto religion. The word *shima*, meaning garden, may have derived from this source.

Shin gyo and *so* an expression to suggest the mixture of formal (*shin*), semi-formal (*gyo*) and informal (*so*) that describes different physical patterns, such as paving, in garden design.

Shinden literally "sleeping hall". The main residence at the centre of the pond gardens of the Heian period.

Shinto the native animistic religion of Japan.

Shishi-odoshi a deer scarer. A bamboo device that repeatedly fills with water, then tips and smacks against a rock.

Shogun military leader. It literally means "barbarian-quelling general".

Shoin **architecture** the style of architecture developed in Japan during the Muromachi (1393–1568) period that included a study room.

Soan the rustic style of architecture of tea houses.

Sode-gaki sleeve fences. Small sections of bamboo and rush fences that divide up views of the garden from the house.

Sumeru originally a Hindu mountain (Meru) that became Mount Shumisen to the Japanese Buddhists.

Tatami the woven rush matting that was especially favoured for the floor of Japanese tea houses.

Tokonoma the alcove in a tea house.

Tsubo-niwa a courtyard garden.

Tsukubai a low basin found by the path to the tea house, usually accompanied by a lantern.

Tsuru-shima see Crane island.

Turtle island derived from the myth of the Mystic Isles, which were said to float on the backs of turtles. Turtle islands (*kame-shima*) are abstract rock arrangements with flippers and heads suggested.

Wabi-sabi can be literally interpreted as "withered loneliness". An aesthetic term that was originally used in poetry, and later came to describe aspects of the tea ceremony, including its pottery, gardens and architecture.

Yatsuhashi an eight-plank zigzag bridge that crosses over streams and ponds which are often planted with irises.

Yugen literally meaning "too deep to see", suggesting a mystery or depth that goes beyond what can be seen. A quality sought by Japanese artists of all kinds, including garden makers.

Zen Buddhism a form of Buddhism introduced to Japan from China in the 13th century. Zen heavily influenced the arts, especially gardens such as the *kare-sansui* and tea garden.

Index

Above: *A dry garden at the Canadian Embassy in Tokyo.*

Above: *Dry garden at Tenju-an, Kyoto.*

Above: *The Zen garden atTenju-an, Kyoto*

Above: *Japanese black pines in the Huntington Botanical Gardens.*

AUTHOR'S ACKNOWLEDGEMENTS
 would specially like to thank David
Greatorex, Roger Midgley; Anna Laflin;
and my wife Anne. I would also like to
thank Masahiro Takaishi, creator of the
Japanese garden in Holland Park. Also to
Marc Keane who included me in his
group of volunteers, weeding and tidying
the gardens of Hakusa-sonso. Thanks to
Gunter Nitschke for his discussions on
the philosophies of Zen and gardens. A
special thanks to Egami and his wife
Hiromi. Thanks also to Joho Ozeki for his
hospitality at the Jiko-in Zen Temple in
Nara; and Venetia Stanley-Smith and to
her husband Tadashi, a few of whose
photographs adorn the pages of
this book.

PUBLISHER'S ACKNOWLEDGEMENTS
The publisher would like to thank the
following for kindly allowing photography
to take place in their gardens: Stella Hore
of the Japanese Garden and Bonsai
Nursery, St Mawgan, Cornwall; Frances
Rasch at Heale Garden and Plant Centre,
Salisbury, Wiltshire; the Japanese-style
roof, Brunei Gallery, School of Oriental and
African Studies, London; the Royal Botanic
Gardens in Kew, London; Newstead Abbey,
Newstead Abbey Park, Nottinghamshire;
the Pureland Zen Garden,
Nottinghamshire; the Tully Japanese
Garden, courtesy of The Irish National
Stud Co., Tully, Co. Kildare, Ireland;
Helmut Kern at Stadt Karlsruhe, Karlsruhe,
Germany; Stadt Augsburg (Augsburg
Botanic Garden) in Germany; the Bonn

Japanese Garden in Rheinaue Park,
Nordrhein-Westfalen, Germany; Lisa
Blackburn at The Huntington Library, Art
Collections and Botanical Gardens, San
Marino CA 91108; Kazuo Tamura of
Tatsumura Silk Company for his garden of
Syoko-ho-en; and to the other temples and
gardens in Japan who kindly gave us
permission to take photographs: Byodo-in,
Hakusa sonso, the Heian Shrine, Honen-in,
Isui-en, Kinkaku-ji, Koetsu-ji, Konchi-in,
Koto-in, Murin-an, Nanzen-ji, Nigo Caste,
Ryogen-in, Sanzen-in, Shoden-ji, Tenju-an,
Tofuku-Ji and Toji-in.

PICTURE ACKNOWLEDGEMENTS
The majority of the photographs in this
book were taken by Alex Ramsay, with
images of materials and equipment taken
by Peter Anderson. A large selection were
provided from Charles Chesshire's
collection. Thanks also to Peter Busby,
who very kindly gave us access to the late
Maureen Busby's extensive photographic
record of garden projects. All
photographs are © Anness Publishing Ltd
unless stated otherwise. The photograph
on p31 (© Anness Publishing) shows
Maureen Busby's 'Shizen' Japanese garden
at Chelsea Flower Show 2004.

   The publisher would like to thank the
following for allowing their photographs
to be reproduced (t = top; b = bottom; c =
centre; r = right; l = left) Alamy Images:
p35b (Takashi Yamaguchi), p39b (Paul
Shawcross), p68t (Photo Japan), p69t
(Photo Japan), p83tm (John Glover),

p86b (Iain Masterton), p95b (Jon
Arnold), p96b (John Glover), p119t
(VisualJapan), p119bl (Claire Takacs),
p120r (John Glover), p121t (Paolo Neri),
p131tr (John Lander); The Bridgeman
Art Library: p10b (Leeds Museums and
Galleries UK); 13b (Tokyo National
Museum, Japan), p15t (Tokyo Fuji Art
Museum, Tokyo, Japan); Harpur Garden
Images: p57tr; istock: p83tl (Maurice van
der Velden), p83tr (Daniel González
Acuna), p104 (Pierre Yu), p124–5
(Michael Irwin), p124 (Martin Mette);
Peter Busby: p37t, p66t, p69bl, 144t,
p154t, p155t, p155b, p168t; Charles
Chesshire: p11b, p12t, p12b, p16t, p20,
p22t, p26t, p26b, 27tl, 27b, p37b, p38t,
p38b, p41, p42t, p42br, p48t, p50b, p57t,
p57b, p60b, p62tl, p66b, p67t, p67br,
p69br, p75t, p76b, p77, p80bl, p98t,
p105t, p105b, p106t, p110b, p121bl,
p121bm, p121br, 138t, 138b, 139t, 142t,
145b; Corbis: p131tm (M. Yamashita), ;
Getty: p131tl (Kaz Chiba), p139t (Umon
Fukushima); Karlsruhe Japanese Garden:
p6, p19, p24t, p25b, p95b; Tadashi
Kajiyana p24b; Werner Forman Archive:
p22b (Burke Collection, New York).

PUBLISHER'S NOTE
Although the advice and information in
this book are believed to be accurate and
true at the time of going to press, neither
the authors nor the publisher can accept
any legal responsibility or liability for
any errors or omissions that may be
made.